Middle East
Country Studies

Reproducible

**Maps,
Facts,
Histories &
Questions**

Written By
RANDY L. WOMACK, M.Ed.
Learning Disabilities & Behavior Disorders
Illustrated By
CHRISTINA "Chris" LEW

Cover Design: **WOMACK & LEW**

A golden educational center publication

P.O. Box 12
Bothell, WA 98041-0012

To Teachers and Parents

This book, *Middle East Country Studies*, was written as a simplified, yet complete, resource book for you to use. The activities can be used as a supplemental resource for your regular history, social studies and/or geography curriculum. It is also a great overview to use when teaching foreign languages.

There are eighteen separate sections in this book. The first seventeen sections are about the independent countries in the Middle East. Each of the countries has a large 8 1/2 x 11" map, one page of current facts/information sheet (1991 Almanac statistics), a short one or two page history through independence and one page of review questions. There are also bonus activities/questions that some of your students can do with another resource book. The eighteenth section is an answer key for the review questions.

New vocabulary words are introduced at the beginning of each section. Within the text they are printed in **bold letters**. If your students are capable of looking up the words in a dictionary, please have them do so. You might even have them use the words in their own sentences. It is suggested that you, as the teacher, go over the words with your students <u>before</u> the lessons are actually begun, making sure that the meanings are understood by the children. This will help your students grasp the concepts being taught.

The following page, "Important Information," can be given to your students to read. We think it is important to teach students why historical events took place and what the people were doing. It seems to help make the events more important to them. We hope you can elaborate on our brief historical discussions. This part of the world is constantly in the news, and our historical overviews should act as a catalyst to study present-day events and attitudes in this region of the world. □

If you are interested in studying the countries of North America, South America, or Far East in the same easy-to-read format as this book, contact your local retail outlet for our books with the same titles. If your retail outlet does not carry the books, contact Golden Educational Center to receive ordering information.

gOldEN EdUCATiONAl CENTER
P.O. Box 12 • Bothell, Washington, 98041
(206) 481-1395

Copyright © 1991 *Golden Educational Center*
All rights reserved - Printed in U.S.A.
Published by Golden Educational Center
P.O. Box 12
Bothell, Washington 98041- 0012

ISBN 1-565000-024-2

EXTRA INFORMATION

The region known today as the *Middle East* is located where the three continents of Asia, Africa and Europe meet. These continents make up most of the Eastern Hemisphere — thus the region came to be called the Middle East. It is important not to stereotype the people who live in this area of the world. This part of the world has a rich and wonderful history. Some of the mightiest, wealthiest and very knowledgeable kingdoms rose, flourished and died in this part of the world.

Throughout history, this part of the world has been torn with war, hatred, conflicts and catastrophes. Much of the unrest comes from the differences of religious beliefs by the various peoples living throughout the area. Even today, there is a tremendous amount of unrest in the region. Pick up any newspaper, magazine, or watch any newscast and you will most likely hear reference to one or more of the nations in the Middle East. We hope someday the Arab, Israeli, and Christian nations and people will be able to live in peace and understanding in the Middle East.

While you read the short histories about the countries and people in this book, please keep in mind that people make history, not facts, dates or even the events themselves. Historical events are a result of people's individual and social attitudes, beliefs and practices. Only when people change their attitudes and beliefs will a history be written without war, destruction and hatred. As you read the histories of the nations in this book, try to relate their histories to what you hear in today's news about those countries.

It is my hope that you learn something from this book so you can be part of a future history book that will tell how people were respected, and even admired, for their individual differences.

Randy L. Womack
Author

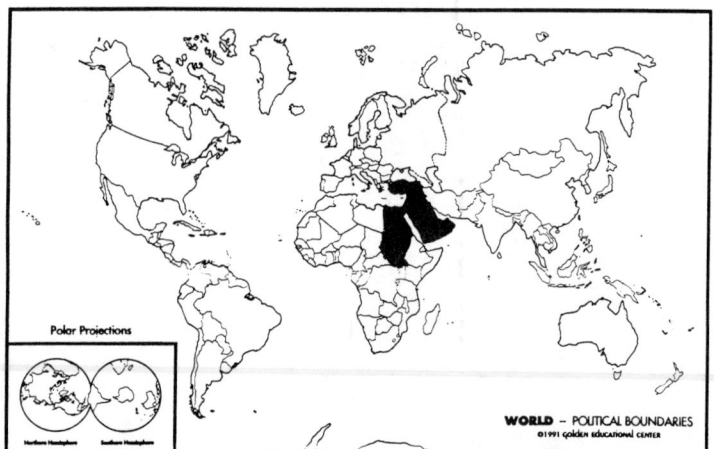

Polar Projections

Northern Hemisphere   Southern Hemisphere

WORLD – POLITICAL BOUNDARIES
©1991 Golden Educational Center

MIDDLE EAST

MIDDLE EAST: **POLITICAL BOUNDARIES**

© GOLDEN EDUCATIONAL CENTER

Middle East

Section Contents

Bahrain

Map • Facts • History & Review Questions

New Words to Learn:

Find the words in a dictionary and write the meanings on the lines.

1. **Arab** - _____

2. **civilization** - _____

3. **monarchy** - _____

4. **Persia** - _____

5. **protectorate** - _____

6. **reform** - _____

7. **social** - _____

8. **welfare** - _____

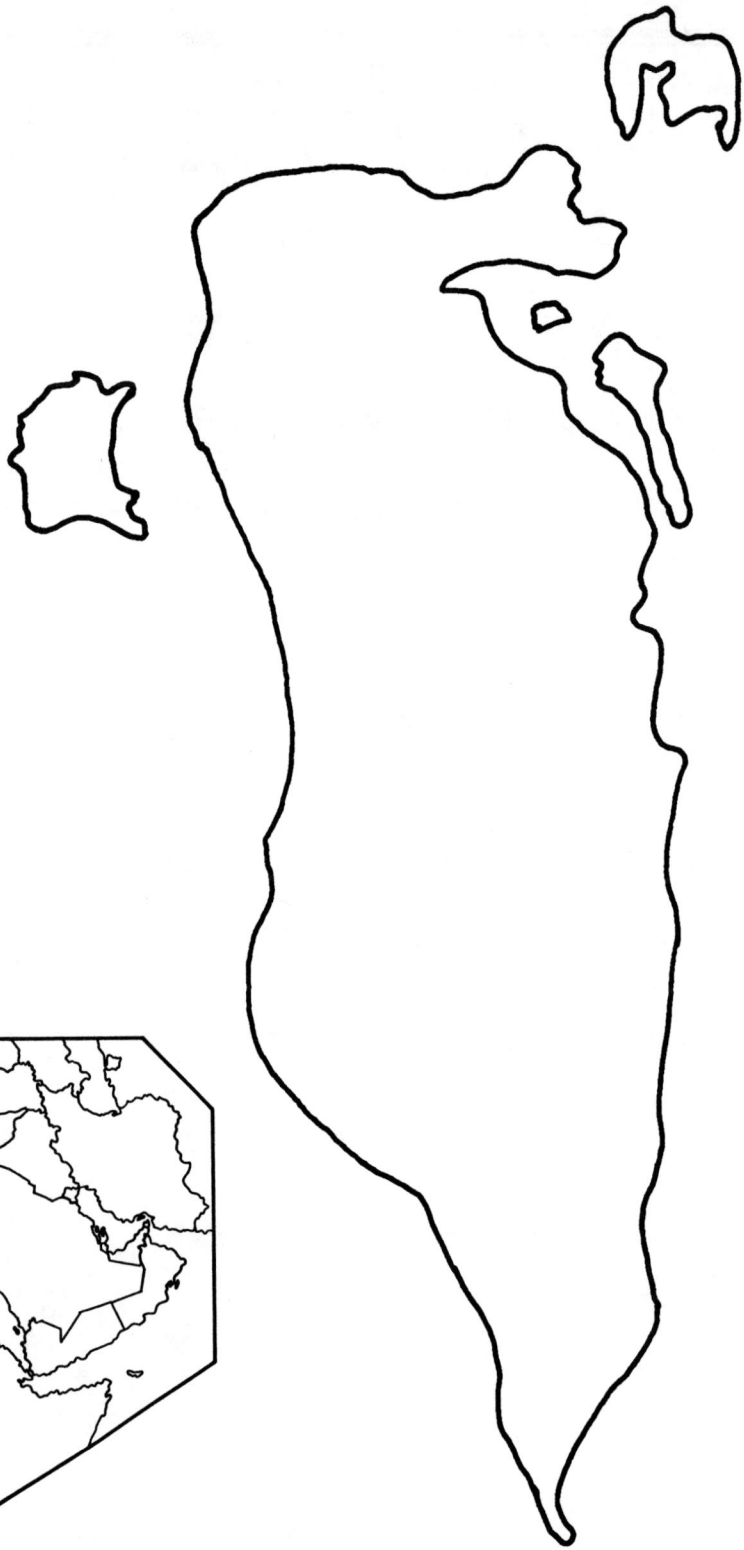

BAHRAIN

BAHRAIN
(bah RAYN)

DATE of INDEPENDENCE: 1971.

NATION'S CAPITAL CITY: Manama.

OFFICIAL LANGUAGE: Arabic.

FORM of GOVERNMENT: Traditional **Monarchy.**

AREA: 258 square miles   (668 square kilometers).

POPULATION (est.1988): 512,000 people.   _Density_: 1985 people per square mile.
766 people per square kilometer.
78% urban (city) living and 22% rural (country) living.

LARGEST CITY: Manama - 146,000 people.

ELEVATION: _Highest_ - Jabal and Dukhan, 443 feet (135 m).
Lowest: Sea level.

ADDITIONAL INFORMATION: The country of Bahrain is made up of one larger island with more than thirty smaller islands. Most of the islands are desert areas. • It has been a major center for trade in the Persian Gulf region for many centuries. • The country was underdeveloped until the discovery of oil in 1932. Today, Bahrain has one of the highest standards of living in the entire gulf region. • Islam is the national religion. Most of the people are Moslems. • Newspapers and magazines are printed in Arabic as well as English.

Bahrain's Flag

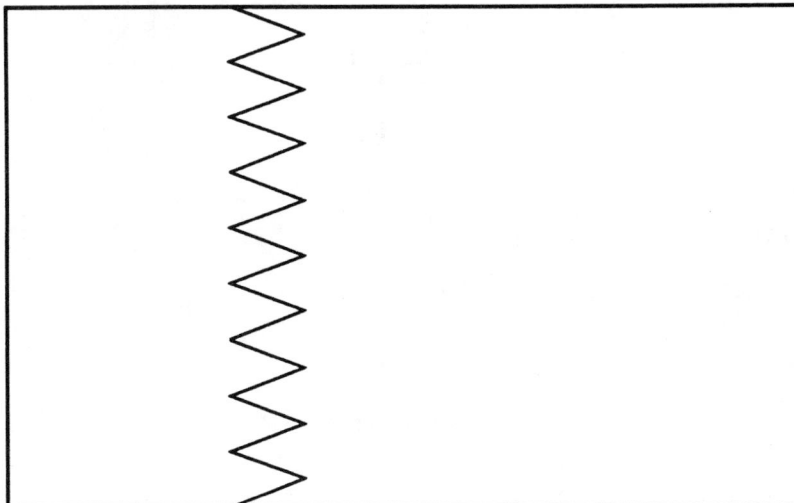

Flag Description

1. The left portion of the flag is white.
2. The right portion of the flag is red.
3. Color the flag the correct colors.

BAHRAIN

Name _____

Date _____

EARLY HISTORY in BRIEF

Bahrain is an island country in the Persian Gulf. It is located off the eastern coast of Saudi Arabia. The country has been a major trade and communications center in the Persian Gulf for many centuries. From as early as 2000 B.C. TO 1800 B.C., Bahrain (then called Dilmaun) was a very prosperous trading **civilization**.

Portugal controlled all of the small country in the 1500's. However, **Persia** (present-day Iran) gained control of Bahrain. They controlled the island until 1782, when a group of Al Khalifah **Arabs**, from Saudi Arabia, drove the Persians from the island. The Al Khalifah Arabs have ruled the country ever since.

In the early 1800's, Great Britain became interested in Bahrain. The British government realized Bahrain's location was excellent for trade in the Persian Gulf region. British forces helped the Bahrainis fight invaders from both Turkey and Saudi Arabia. In 1861, Bahrain became a British **protectorate**. Bahrain gave Great Britain control of its foreign affairs in return for Britain's protection.

Bahrain became the first Middle East country to establish **social welfare** programs. It developed the programs during the 1920's and 1930's. Under the programs, the government built hospitals and schools. However, the country remained underdeveloped until oil was discovered on the island's mainland in 1932.

The people of Bahrain demanded more direct say in the country's governmental affairs in the late 1940's and early 1950's. As a result of wide-spread rioting that took place in 1956, minor political **reforms** were made in the government.

In 1971, Great Britain withdrew its control over much of the Persian Gulf region. Later that same year, Bahrain gained its independence. It soon joined the Arab League and the United Nations.

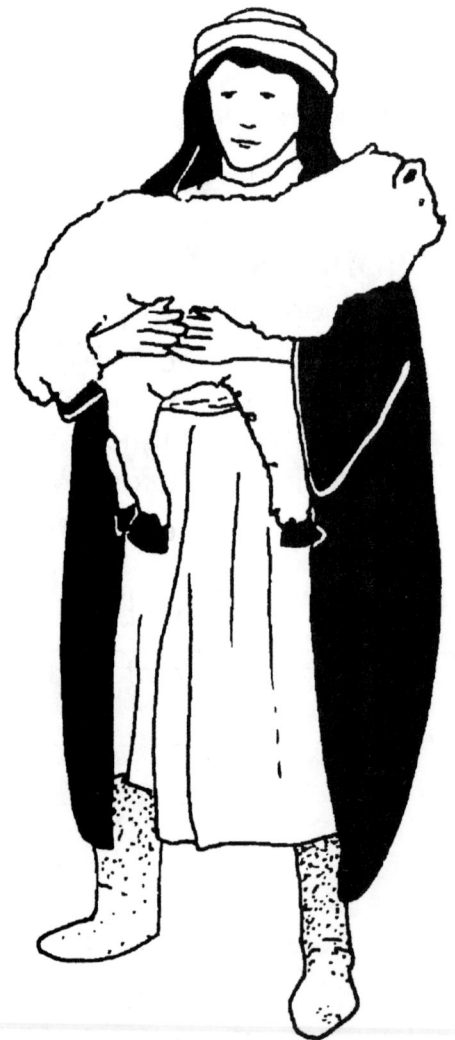

❏ ❏ ❏ ❏ ❏

A shepherd carries a lamb.

MIDDLE EAST: **Section** 1 - 4

© GOLDEN EDUCATIONAL CENTER

BAHRAIN

REVIEW QUESTIONS

Circle each correct answer.

1. Bahrain became totally independent in ...
   a. 1971   b. 1800   c. 1782   d. 1956

2. Bahrain was first controlled by ...
   a. Saudi Arabia   b. Persia   c. Portugal   d. Great Britain

3. Until 1782, the region was controlled by ...
   a. Saudi Arabia   b. Persia   c. Portugal   d. Great Britain

Fill in each blank with the correct answer.

4. From what country did Bahrain gain its independence? _____

5. The capital city of Bahrain is _____ .

6. _____ was the first European country to control Bahrain.

7. The people wanted more _____ in the government in the late 1940's and early 1950's.

8. Who has ruled Bahrain ever since Persia? _____

9. Bahrain became the first Middle East country to establish _____ .

10. In 1861, Bahrain became a British _____ .

11. Explain why Great Britain took an interest in Bahrain in the early 1800's.

   _____

   _____

   _____

Bonus ☆ ☆ ☆

   Use another resource book and write a report on the Al Khalifah Arabs, Persian Gulf, British Protectorates, Arab League of Nations, or Bahrain's political reforms of 1956. Include pictures and maps in your report if they are applicable.

Cyprus

Map • Facts • History & Review Questions

New Words to Learn:

Find the words in a dictionary and write the meanings on the lines.

1. **ancestry** - _____

2. **ancient** - _____

3. **century** - _____

4. **city-state** - _____

5. **conquer** - _____

6. **constitution** - _____

7. **descent** - _____

8. **empire** - _____

9. **native** - _____

10. **political** - _____

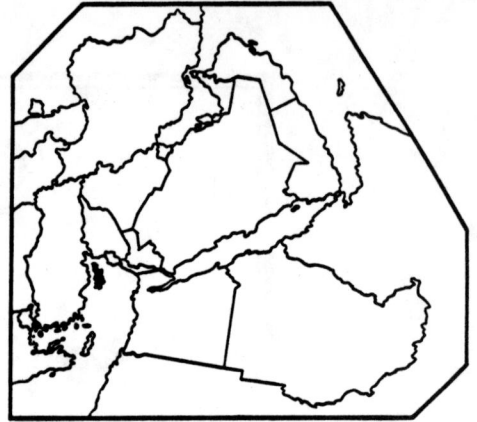

CYPRUS

CYPRUS

(SY pruhs)

DATE of INDEPENDENCE: August 16, 1960.

NATION'S CAPITAL CITY: Nicosia.

OFFICIAL LANGUAGE: Greek.

FORM of GOVERNMENT: Republic.

AREA: 3,572 square miles (9,251 square kilometers).

POPULATION (est.1989): 708,000 people. *Density*: 198 people per square mile.
76 people per square kilometer.
58% urban (city) living and 42% rural (country) living.

LARGEST CITY: Nicosia - 124,300 people.

ELEVATION: *Highest*: Mount Olympus - 6,403 feet (1,952 m) above sea level.
Lowest: Sea level.

ADDITIONAL INFORMATION: Cyprus is part of the Asian continent. However, the people live more like European people than Asian people. • Eighty percent of the people are of Greek origin. The other twenty percent are of Turkish origin. • The island country's official name is *Kypriaki Dimokratia* (in Greek) and *Kibris Cumhuriyeiti* (in Turkish). Both names mean *Republic of Cyprus*. • According to its constitution, the president must be a Greek Cypriot, elected by Greek Cypriots. The vice-president must be a Turkish Cypriot, elected by Turkish Cypriots.

Cyprus' Flag

Flag Description

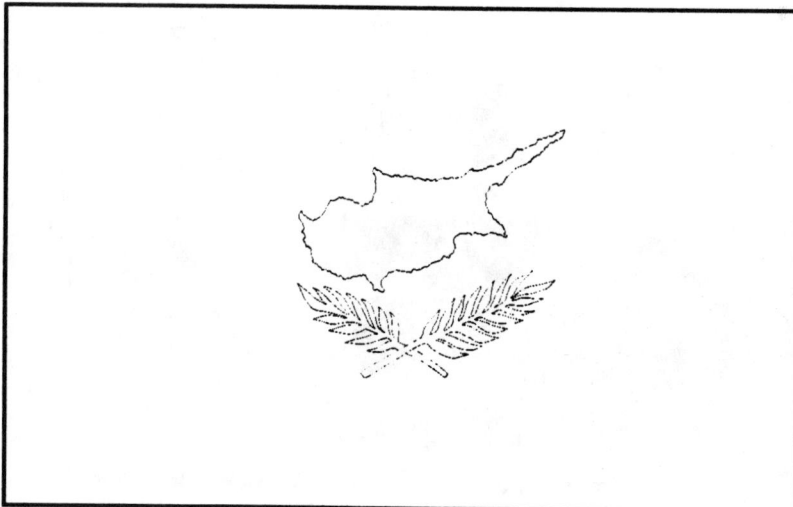

1. The background of the flag is white.

2. The map of Cyprus is a copper-yellow color, which represents copper.

3. The two crossed green olive branches represent peace.

4. Color the flag the correct colors.

© GOLDEN EDUCATIONAL CENTER

CYPRUS

Name _____

Date _____

EARLY HISTORY in BRIEF

Cyprus in an island country in the northeast corner of the Mediterranean Sea. It is located approximately 40 miles south of Turkey and 60 miles west of Syria.

It is estimated the earliest known people to live on the island arrived around 6000 B.C. Greek settlers came to Cyprus about 1200 B.C. The Greek settlers established **city-states** like the ones in **ancient** Greece.

Over the **centuries**, the island of Cyprus has been **conquered** by numerous nations. Before the time of Christ, the Assyrians, Egyptians, Persians, Greeks and Romans all conquered and ruled the small country. Saint Paul and Saint Barnabas brought the message of **Christianity** to the island in A.D. 45. About three hundred years later, Cyprus became part of the Byzantine **Empire**. The island was conquered by England in 1191, and then sold to a French nobleman. Ottoman Turks captured Cyprus in the 1570's. They ruled the island until 1878, when they turned it over to Great Britain.

In the 1950's, the people of Cyprus with Greek **ancestry** started a movement to unite Greece and Cyprus as one country. These Greek Cypriots started attacking British holdings on the island. In 1959, Greece and Turkey met and agreed that Cyprus should become an independent nation. Great Britain accepted their agreement and granted Cyprus its independence on August 16, 1960. Its **constitution** was written by Greece, Turkey and Great Britain.

Today, there is **political** unrest in Cyprus. Greek and Turkish Cypriots have met several times since 1974 in an effort to rewrite Cyprus' constitution. However, they have yet to reach an agreement.

Most of the people living in the country of Cyprus consider themselves either Greek or Turkish Cypriots. Very few of them think of themselves as **native** to the island of Cyprus. About four-fifths of today's population are of Greek origin. Most of the other people in Cyprus are of Turkish **descent**.

❏ ❏ ❏ ❏ ❏

Two monks of St. Barnabas's Monastary paint icons.

CYPRUS

REVIEW QUESTIONS   Date _____

Circle each correct answer.

1. The official language of Cyprus is ...
    a. Greek   b. English   c. Turkish   d. Cyprusese

2. Very few of the people living in Cyprus consider themselves as ...
    a. Greek   b. Turkish   c. Native   d. British

3. Cyprus gained its independence in ...
    a. 1570   b. 1950   c. 1959   d. 1960

Fill in each blank with the correct answer.

4. The _____ came to Cyprus about _____ .

5. Cyprus is located in the _____ _____ .

6. Today, there is _____ _____ in Cyprus.

7. Cyprus has a _____ form of government.

8. Cyprus' largest city, according to population, is _____ .

9. The island was _____ by England in _____ . It was then
    _____ to a _____ nobleman.

10. What did Saints Paul and Barnabas bring to Cyprus? _____

11. Cyprus' _____ was written by_____ ,
    _____ , and _____ _____ .

12. Explain why the people with Greek ancestory attacked British holdings in the 1950's.

    _____

    _____

Bonus ☆ ☆ ☆

Use another resource book and write a report on the Mediterranean Sea, Ancient Greece,
Great Britain's Empire, Ottoman Turks, Christianity, St. Paul, or St. Barnabas.
Include pictures and maps in your report if they are applicable.

Egypt

Map • Facts • History & Review Questions

New Words to Learn:

Find the words in a dictionary and write the meanings on the lines.

1. **chamber** - _____

2. **convert** - _____

3. **humanity** - _____

4. **irrigation** - _____

5. **isthmus** - _____

6. **magnificent** - _____

7. **precious** - _____

8. **pharaoh** - _____

9. **pyramid** - _____

10. **savage** - _____

11. **tomb** - _____

EGYPT

EGYPT
(EE jipt)

Name _____

Date _____

DATE of INDEPENDENCE: 1922.

NATION'S CAPITAL CITY: Cairo.

OFFICIAL LANGUAGE: Arabic.

FORM of GOVERNMENT: Republic.

AREA: 386,650 square miles (1,001,418 square kilometers).

POPULATION (est.1989)**:** 54,139,000 people.   *Density*: 140 people per square mile.
54 people per square kilometer.
44% urban (city) living and 56% rural (country) living.

LARGEST CITY: Cairo - 6,305,000 people.

ELEVATION: *Highest*: Jabal Katrinah - 8,668 feet (2,642 m) above sea level.
Lowest: Sea level.

ADDITIONAL INFORMATION: Egypt is located mostly in the continent of Africa. However, a small portion of it, the Sinai Peninsula, is in Asia. • Most of the country is covered with deserts. One is the Sahara Desert and it is the largest in the world. • The Nile River supplies almost all of the country's water. • Farming employs more people than any other occupation. • Ninety-nine percent of the population live on 3½ percent of the country's land — along the Nile River or the Suez Canal.
• Egypt is the second most populated country of Africa.

Egypt's Flag

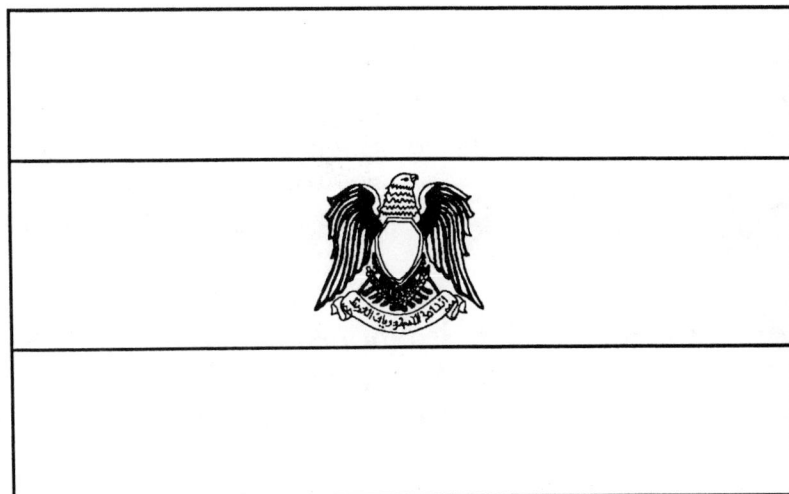

Flag Description

1. The top stripe is red and stands for sacrifice.

2. The bottom stripe is black and represents the past; while the center white stripe symbolizes purity.

3. The gold hawk emblem in the center of the flag was the mark of the tribe of Mohammed, the founder of Islam. (Several other Arab nations have similar flags.)

4. Color the flag the correct colors.

EGYPT

Name _____

Date _____

EARLY HISTORY in BRIEF

Egypt is considered by many historians as the *birthplace of civilization*. However, Egypt did not develop as a nation until 3100 B.C. It had been divided into small states that eventually combined into two states. The two states included *Upper* and *Lower Egypt*. Historians believe that Upper Egypt conquered Lower Egypt in 3100 B.C., and united the two states. However, the ancient Egyptian people still called their country the *Two Lands*.

The ancient Egyptians lived colorful, active lives. Many of them were creative artists, skilled craftsmen and even explorers. The Egyptian armies were the most powerful and well trained in the known world. They were among the first people to search for answers concerning **humanity**, nature and God. However, they looked on other people as **savages**, and enslaved tens of thousands of the people they conquered.

The Nile River was at the very center of their life and survival. Each year the mighty river would flood the lands and deposit rich, fertile soil along its banks, all the way to the edge of the desert. Egyptian farmers planted their crops in the rich, black soil along the Nile.

Religion was emphasized by the ancient Egyptians. The great **pyramids** were built by the Egyptian **pharaohs** at the edge of the desert. They were built as **tombs** for the pharaohs. It was their religious belief that a man's body had to be preserved and protected in order for his soul to live forever. They would bury the pharaoh's body beneath the pyramid, or inside a secret **chamber** within the pyramid. They also buried treasures of gold and other **precious** objects within secret chambers. It is thought that riches were buried with the pharaohs because they would need the objects in their afterlife. Many historians believe the shape of the pyramids had a religious meaning to the builders.

The **magnificent** ancient Egyptian civilization lasted about 2,500 years before finally being divided and eventually conquered by other nations.

From about 1100 B.C. to A.D. 639, when Arabs invaded Egypt, the country was conquered and occupied by several different peoples. In 642, Moslem troops from Arabia finally took control of Alexandria, the capital of Egypt. At that time, Egypt was part of the Eastern Roman Empire (Byzantine Empire). The Arab Empire ruled Egypt for the next 200 years. Over that period of time, most of the Egyptian people were **converted** from the Christian religion to the religion of Islam (the Moslem Religion). The people also began speaking Arabic, the Arabs' language.

Moslem (also Muslim) rulers in Baghdad (the capital of their empire) began to loosen control of their territories in the mid-800's. From the mid-800's to the mid-900's, two Turkish dynasties governed Egypt almost independently from the Moslem leaders.

EGYPT

Name _____

Date _____

In 969, the Fatimite dynasty of North Africa conquered and ruled Egypt. They were at odds with the Moslem leaders in Baghdad, because the Fatimites founded the Islamic religion. The Fatimites established Cairo as their capital city, and started the University of Al-Azhar. Cairo developed into one of the important cities of the Moslem world.

During the 1180's, the Fatimite leaders were fearful that Christian troops would invade them from Jerusalem. The Christian forces had recently captured the holy city of Jerusalem from the Moslems in the First Crusade.

It was in 1517, that the Turks conquered Egypt and added it to their Ottoman Empire. In 1798, French soldiers invaded Egypt in order to gain control of the land route to the British colony of India. France's Emperor, Napoleon, captured the city of Alexandria. In 1801, British and Ottoman troops drove the French out of Egypt.

In 1799, a soldier in the army of Napoleon Bonaparte, who was then on a military expedition in Egypt, found the Rosetta Stone. The stone had three different languages carved on it. Each language reported the same message. This allowed the translation of the hieroglyphs by comparing it with the known Greek words.

In 1807, Muhammid Ali, drove the British out of Egypt. He introduced commercial growing of cotton in Egypt. He built a dam near Cairo, as well as **irrigation** canals in the Nile Delta. He controlled Egypt's agriculture, industry and trade. Muhammid Ali also built schools, a modern army and navy, and won victories in Arabia, Greece, Sudan, and Syria.

In 1859, the Suez Canal began to be built through the **Isthmus** of Suez. It took ten years to complete the enormous project. The completion of the Suez Canal shortened the route from the Mediterranean Sea to the Indian Ocean by thousands of miles and several days.

Britain gained control of Egypt after World War I. The British gave Egypt its independence in 1922.

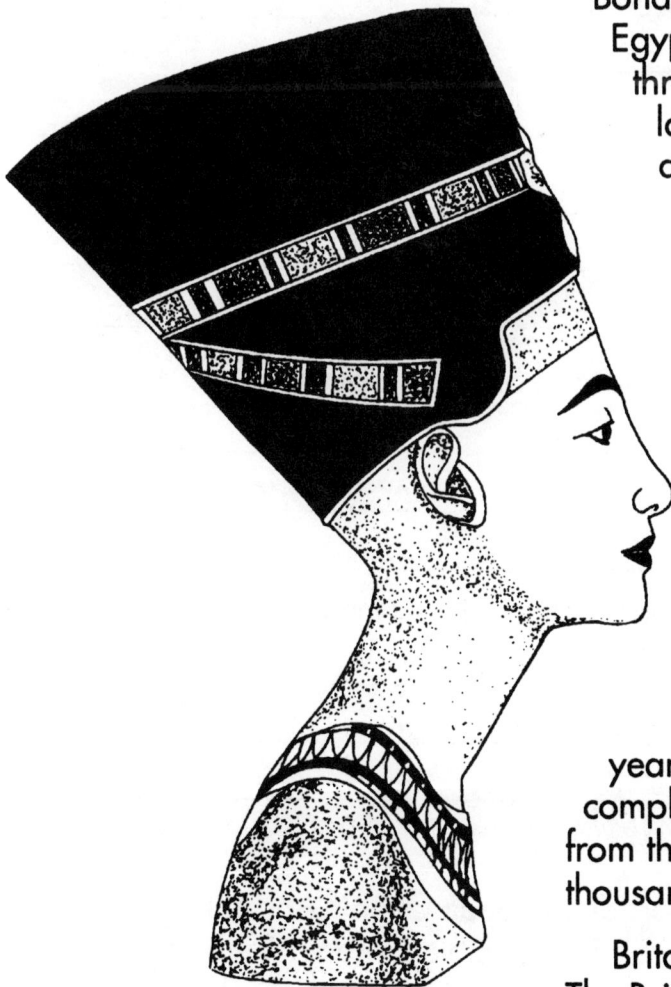

Queen Nefertiti's name means "beautiful head."

❏ ❏ ❏ ❏ ❏ ❏ ❏ ❏ ❏

EGYPT

Name _____

REVIEW QUESTIONS   **Date** _____

Fill in each blank with the correct answer.

1. Egypt is sometimes considered the _____ .

2. The two states in Egypt were called _____ and _____ .

3. According to population, _____ is the largest city in Egypt.

4. Egyptian pharaohs built _____ near the edge of the _____
   They were built as _____ for the _____ .

5. In what year did Britain give modern Egypt its independence? _____

6. The ancient Egyptian _____ were the most _____
   and well trained in the known _____ .

7. In 1807, Muhammid Ali introduced _____ _____
   growing in Egypt. He also drove the _____ out of the region.
   Muhammid Ali also built a _____ near _____ and
   _____ _____ in the Nile _____ .

8. Explain why the pharaohs were buried with gold and precious objects.

   _____

   _____

   _____

9. Explain why the building of the Suez Canal was (and still is) so important.

   _____

   _____

   _____

Bonus ☆ ☆ ☆

   Use another resource book and write a report on the Suez Canal, Ancient Egypt,
Hieroglyphics, Rosetta Stone, Pyramids, Islam, Christianity, Napoleon, Muhammid Ali,
World War I, or a Pharaoh. See if you can also find current information about Egypt
in the newspaper. Include pictures and maps in your report if they are applicable.

Iran

Map • Facts • History & Review Questions

New Words to Learn:

Find the words in a dictionary and write the meanings on the lines.

1. **architecture** - _____

2. **barren** - _____

3. **fertile** - _____

4. **influence** - _____

5. **Isalm** - _____

6. **neglect** - _____

7. **nobles** - _____

8. **standardize** - _____

9. **stylize** - _____

10. **technology** - _____

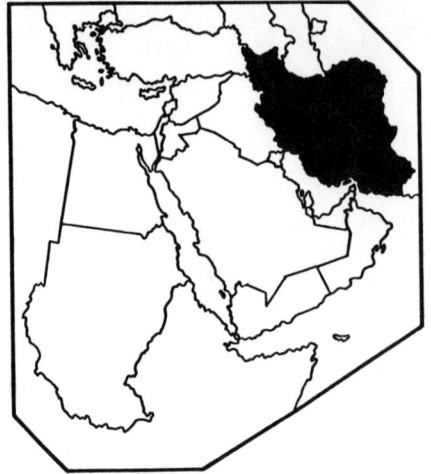

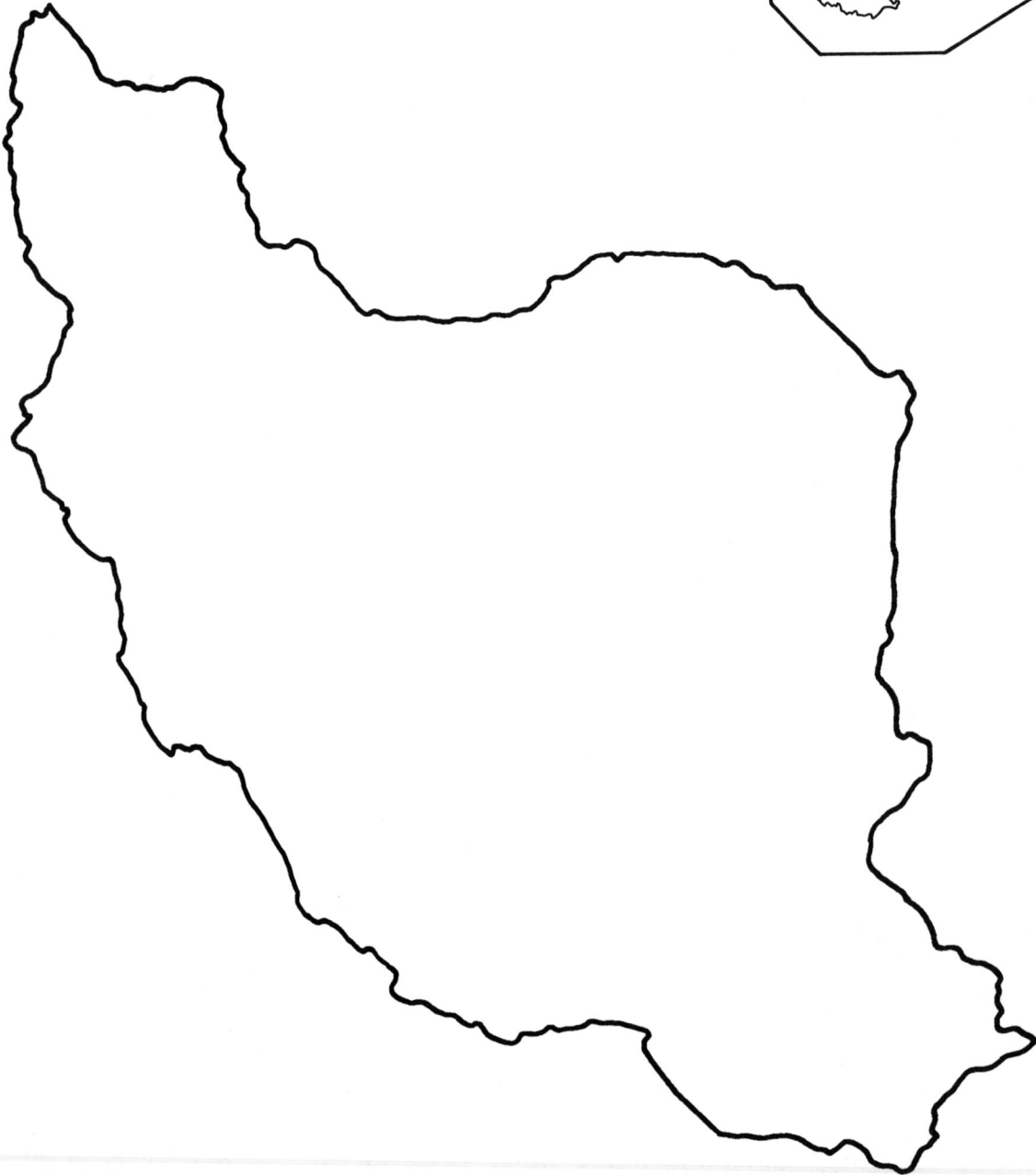

IRAN

IRAN

(ee RAHN)

DATE of INDEPENDENCE: Always Independent.

NATION'S CAPITAL CITY: Teheran.

OFFICIAL LANGUAGE: Farsi (also known as Persian).

FORM of GOVERNMENT: Islamic Republic.

AREA: 636,293 square miles   (1,647,991 square kilometers).

POPULATION (est. 1989): 3,000,000 people.   _Density:_ 5 people per square mile.
2 people per square kilometer.
48% urban (city) living and 52% rural (country) living.

LARGEST CITY: Teheran - 6,022,000 people.

ELEVATION: _Highest:_ Mt. Damavand - 18,386 feet (5,604 m) above sea level.
Lowest: Caspian Sea Coast - 90 feet (27 meters) below sea level.

ADDITIONAL INFORMATION: Iran's official name is _Islamic Republic of Iran._ • It is one of the oldest countries in the world. • Iran was once part of the great Persian Empire. It lost its wealth and power between the 1200's and 1900's. The irrigation systems crumbled, the land became unproductive and it became a backward nation. • Since the discovery and production of oil, the country has made great strides in its development. • Women do not have the same rights and have less freedom than the Iranian men.

Iran's Flag

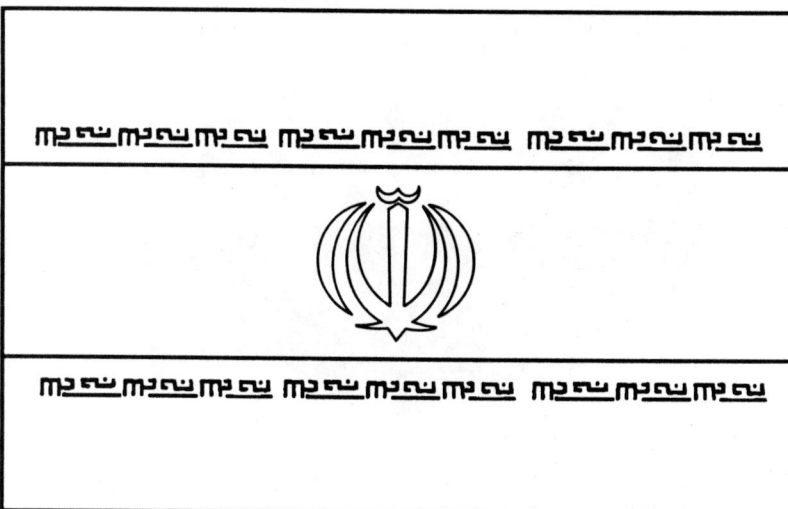

Flag Description

1. The top stripe is green; the center stripe is white; and the bottom stripe is red.

2. The nation's coat of arms is in the center of the flag, and it is green. It is a **stylized** drawing of the word **Allah**, printed in the Arabic language.

3. Color the flag the correct colors.

IRAN

Name _____

Date _____

EARLY HISTORY in BRIEF

Iran is one of the oldest countries in the world. In ancient times, it was the major portion of the country of *Persia* — which comes from the original Greek name of *Persis*. Some people in other countries even today call Iran, Persia. It is also mentioned several times in the *Old Testament* of the Bible.

The earliest known civilization in Persia was that of the Elamites. They came to the area before 1200 B.C. Tribes of Medes and Persians were nomads, and wandered into the area about 900 B.C. They came from the area that today is southern Russia. These nomads were very well organized. The empire they built lasted over 200 years. During the height of their kingdom's power and **influence**, they developed a very good "pony express system" to deliver the mail. They also designed and built an irrigation system. They introduced the first widespread system for using coins for money. The Persians also used a system of **standardized** weights and measures.

The Persians treated their slaves and the people they conquered better than any other earlier rulers. Later leaders built on Persian accomplishments to unify and build their empires.

In the 500's B.C., Persia became the vast center of the Achaemenid Empire. This empire included most of the known world. The vast area extended from northern Africa to southern Europe, to southern Russia, to the Gulf of Oman and to India in the east. The area was almost as big as the present-day United States, which is the fourth largest country in the world. It is amazing that they did this with none of today's communication **technology**.

A coin from Alexander the Great's empire. The front side of the coin, on the left, has a portrait of Alexander.
The reverse side of the coin, on the right, is the goddess Athene holding Nike, symbolizing wisdom, strategy and victory.

IRAN

Name _____

Date _____

Most of the Persia's common people lived in mud huts for houses. They were probably much like the huts you find the country people of Iran living in today. The kings and **nobles** had huge palaces and homes built from stone. Their **architecture** and construction was excellent. Some of the ruins can still be found in Iran today.

In 400 B.C., Persians invaded Greece , but Greece was not overtaken. This defeat ended the empire's expansion. Alexander the Great conquered the empire in 331 B.C.

Arabs came from the west and invaded and conquered Persia (Iran) in A.D. 641. The Arabs were of the **Islam** religion. After the Arab's gained control of Iran, they sent religious leaders from Baghdad and Damascus to rule the country. They ruled Iran for 200 years. During this period, the Arabs converted most of the Iranian people to Islam. Over a period of time, Arabic words and alphabet filtered into the Iranian language. Iran became a world center for art, literature and science.

The Arabic empire crumbled after the 800's. Iran eventually broke up into small kingdoms under several different rulers.

Forces from Turkey conquered most of the Iranian kingdoms in 1037. These Turks ruled the region until 1221. That is the year thousands of Mongols, led by Genghis Khan, invaded Iran. They destroyed many cities and slaughtered thousands of people. The Mongols gained control of Iran in only a short period of time. This conquest began Iran's decline as a world center of education and learning. The irrigation projects built during the Persian Empire were **neglected**. Much of the land that had once been **fertile** farmland became dry and **barren** because the irrigation systems were not taken care of.

During the 1800's and early 1900's, Iran came under the control of Great Britain and Russia. The British wanted control over the area so they could protect India (a British colony) from the French while under Napoleon's leadership, and later from the Russians. Russia wanted control of Iran so they could have a direct route to the Persian Gulf. In 1827, Russian troops conquered Iran and in the treaty they agreed to set Iran's present-day northern boundary.

Many battles were fought on Iranian soil during World War I, even though it remained neutral. Russian and British troops defended oil fields located throughout the country.

Iran wanted to remain neutral in World War II also. However, the Allies needed Iran's oil. The Shah of Iran refused to sell them the oil they needed. British and Russian troops invaded Iran in 1941, and quickly took control of the country and its oil. British and U.S. troops left Iran shortly after World War II. Iran regained control of its oil fields in 1946.

❑ ❑ ❑ ❑ ❑ ❑ ❑ ❑ ❑ ❑ ❑

IRAN

REVIEW QUESTIONS

Circle each correct answer.

1. Iran's main religion is ...
   a. Christianity   b. Atheistic   c. Buddha   d. Islam

2. The official language of Iran is ...
   a. English   b. Arabian   c. Iranian   d. Farsi

3. Today's government of Iran is ...
   a. Democracy   b. Monarchy   c. Islamic Republic   d. Dictatorship

Fill in each blank with the correct answer.

4. The capital city of Iran is _____ . According to
   _____ it is also Iran's _____ city.

5. Medes and Persians built an early _____ that lasted over _____
   years. They developed a system to _____ mail, and the first
   system using _____ for _____ . They also built
   an _____ system.

6. Persians and Medes were _____ .

7. Ancient Iran was mostly the country of _____ . It comes from
   the _____ word _____ .

8. What year did Iran gain its independence? _____

9. Explain why British and Russian troops invaded Iran in 1941.

   _____
   _____
   _____

Bonus ☆ ☆ ☆

Use another resource book and write a report on Persia, the Achaemenid Empire,
Arabs, Alexander the Great, Arabian Empire, Napoleon, or Irrigation Systems.
See if you can also find current information about Iran in the newspaper.
Include pictures and maps in your report if they are applicable.

Iraq

Map • Facts • History & Review Questions

New Words to Learn:

Find the words in a dictionary and write the meanings on the lines.

1. **archeology** - _____

2. **astronomy** - _____

3. **capital** - _____

4. **descendant** - _____

5. **flourish** - _____

6. **historian** - _____

7. **Moslem** - _____

8. **myth** - _____

9. **remnant** - _____

10. **terrace** - _____

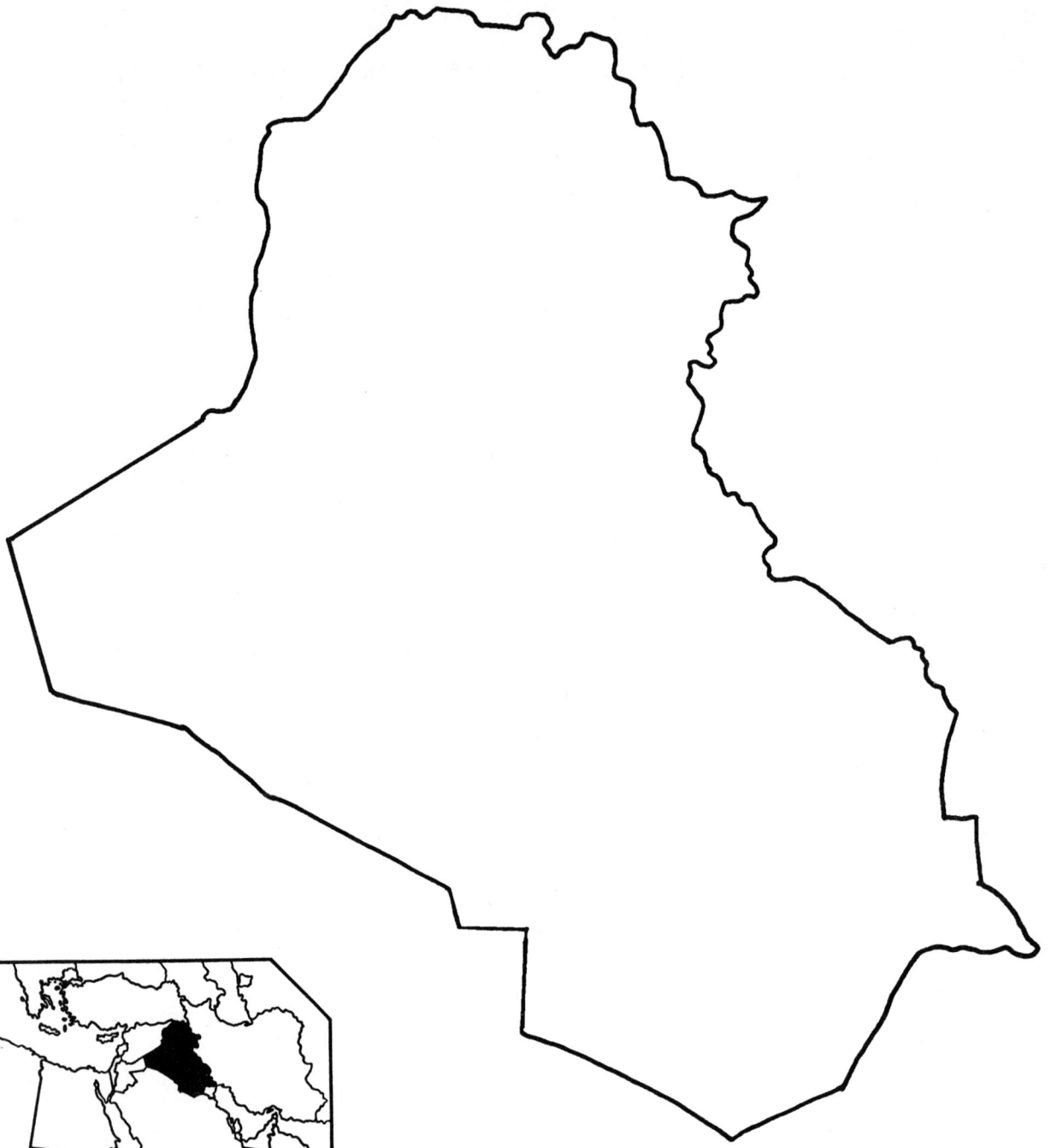

IRAQ

IRAQ

(ee RAHK)

Name _____

Date _____

DATE of INDEPENDENCE: 1932.

NATION'S CAPITAL CITY: Baghdad.

OFFICIAL LANGUAGE: Arabic.

FORM of GOVERNMENT: Republic.

AREA: 167,924 square miles (434,921 square kilometers).

POPULATION (est.1989): 18,782,000 people. _Density_: 112 people per square mile.
43 people per square kilometer.
64% urban (city) living and 36% rural (country) living.

LARGEST CITY: Baghdad - 3,400,000 people.

ELEVATION: _Highest_: Zagros Mountains - 11,840 feet (3,609 m) above sea level.
Lowest: Sea level.

ADDITIONAL INFORMATION: Iraq grows more dates than any other country in the world.
• The ancient Greeks called the region of Iraq _Mesopotamia,_ which means _between the rivers._ • The president of the country is also the head of the armed forces. He is also chairman of the council that makes the government's policies.
• Oil accounts for more than 90% of Iraq's exports and about 60% of the country's income. • Iraqi law requires children from 7 to 12 years old to attend school. Most of the schools are in the city. About 45% of the people can read and write.

Iraq's Flag

Flag Description

1. The top stripe is red and stands for sacrifice.

2. The bottom stripe is black and represents the past; while the center white stripe symbolizes purity. (Several other Arab nations have similar flags.)

3. The stars in the center stripe are green.

4. Color the flag the correct colors.

IRAQ

EARLY HISTORY in BRIEF

Iraq is one of the oldest countries in the world. It was the center of several ancient civilizations, including the Assyrian, Babylonian, Chaldean, and Sumer civilizations. Some historians speculate that the Garden of Eden, mentioned in the book of *Genesis* in the *Old Testament*, might have been located in the region of Iraq.

Assyria was an ancient country that covered the northern part of present-day Iraq. **Historians** know very little about early Assyrian history. The oldest documents discovered to date are dated about 2000 B.C. It is believed that people were in Assyria earlier than any believed to be in Babylonia. **Archeologists** have found **remnants** of items, houses, art (mostly sculpted stone), pottery, and written documents from the ancient Assyrian civilization. They have learned quite a bit about the Assyrian way of life from these items.

Assyrians have been called the *Romans of Asia*. They were called this because, like the Romans, they were great warring people. They conquered their enemies with superb organization, weapons, and equipment.

Written records show that Assyria in 1813 B.C., extended its boundaries and powers. Assyria was then under the control of the Babylonians. It again became an independent country by the mid-1300's B.C. In the 800's B.C., it expanded its empire and became a great power. Assyria's power and greatness declined rapidly after the mid-600's B.C. Attacks from Media and Babylonia in 614 and 612 B.C. ended the Assyrian Empire.

Hammurabi's Code, was the first set of laws in history to be written. They were carved on a stone tablet below a relief of the god giving Hammurabi, the king of Babylon, the laws.

IRAQ

Name _____

Date _____

Babylonia was the ancient region around the Tigris and Euphrates rivers in Mesopotamia (now southern Iraq). The region centered around the ancient city of Babylon, which was located about 60 miles south of present-day Baghdad. The great Babylonian civilization **flourished** in the region from 2700 B.C. and 500 B.C. The Babylonians developed one of the very first known forms of writing, a set of laws, and studies in mathematics, **astronomy**, and other sciences.

The **descendants** of Noah, who settled in the Babylonia region after the Deluge (the flood reported in Genesis, Chapter 11) were the first to settle in the region. They began construction of a **terraced** pyramid tower in the city of Babel — meaning *Gate of God* in Hebrew. The Hebrew word for Babylon is *Babel*. The people started to build a tower that reached the heavens.

The city of Babylon was sometimes referred to as *The Splendid City*. It was one of the greatest cities of the entire ancient world. Babylon was the **capital** city of the ancient kingdom of Babylonia. The city was surrounded by big walls decorated with blue glazed brick and pictures of **mythical** beasts. People entered and left the city through huge bronze gates. The Euphrates River ran through the center of the city.

The Sumerians invaded and controlled Babylonia from about 3000 B.C. to 2400 B.C. They established small, independent city-states throughout the kingdom. The Semites conquered Babylonia in the 2300's B.C. The Elamites invaded the region in a short period of time. This helped the growth of the first Babylonian Empire. The Babylonian civilization reached its greatest heights from 1800 to 1500 B.C. Persian armies conquered the region in 550 B.C., and added it to their vast empire. Alexander the Great took control of the Empire in 331 B.C. The Babylonian Empire crumbled soon after Alexander died.

Arab armies conquered Mesopotamia (Iraq) in A.D. 637. They brought their Arabic language and the **Moslem** religion. Baghdad was made the capital of the Arab Empire from 750 to 1258. Mongols invaded Mesopotamia in the 1200's and destroyed Baghdad. The Ottoman Turks took control of Mesopotamia in 1534.

Britain took the region from the Turks during World War I (1914-1918). The British helped the Mesopotamian leaders set up a government in 1921. The leaders named their nation *Iraq*. British control of Iraq ended in 1932. The League of Nations admitted Iraq to membership as an independent nation.

In 1945, Iraq helped form the Arab League. In 1945, Iraq joined the other members of the Arab League in a war to prevent the creation of Israel. The Israelis defeated the Arab forces, and the nation of Israel was created. Conflict between Arab and Israeli people have continued throughout the ages, and continue even today.

❏ ❏ ❏ ❏ ❏ ❏ ❏ ❏ ❏ ❏ ❏

IRAQ

REVIEW QUESTIONS   Date _____

Circle each correct answer.

1. From which country did Iraq gain its independence?

    a. Spain   b. United States   c. France   d. Great Britain

2. The official language of Iraq is ...

    a. Arabic   b. Iraqi   c. English   d. Islam

3. Iraq is located at the northern end of the ...

    a. Mediterranean Sea   b. Atlantic Ocean   c. Red Sea   d. Persian Gulf

Fill in each blank with the correct answer.

4. In what year did Iraq gain its independence? _____

5. Assyrians have been called the _____.

6. Ancient Babylonia was the region around the _____ and _____ rivers. This area was known as _____ .

7. The first people to settle in the region of Iraq were descendants of _____.

8. The ancient country of _____ covered part of present-day _____.

9. Explain why the Assyrians were called the *Romans of Asia*.

_____

_____

_____

_____

Bonus ☆ ☆ ☆

Use another resource book and write a report on the Euphrates and/or Tigris Rivers, the Assyrian, Babylonian, Chaldean, or Sumer people or civilizations, Noah, the great flood as recorded in *Genesis*, Babylon and/or its Tower of Babel, the Garden of Eden, or astronomy (not astrology). You can also report on the war between Iraq and Iran in the 1980's, or the Iraq – Kuwait War in 1990-91.
See if you can also find current information about Iraq in the newspaper.
Include pictures and maps in your report if they are applicable.

Israel

Map • Facts • History
& Review Questions

New Words to Learn:

Find the words in a dictionary and write the meanings on the lines.

1. **Jesus Christ** - _____

2. **enslave** - _____

3. **exile** - _____

4. **Hebrew** - _____

5. **Judaism** - _____

6. **persecute** - _____

7. **sacred** - _____

8. **slaughter** - _____

9. **tallith** - _____

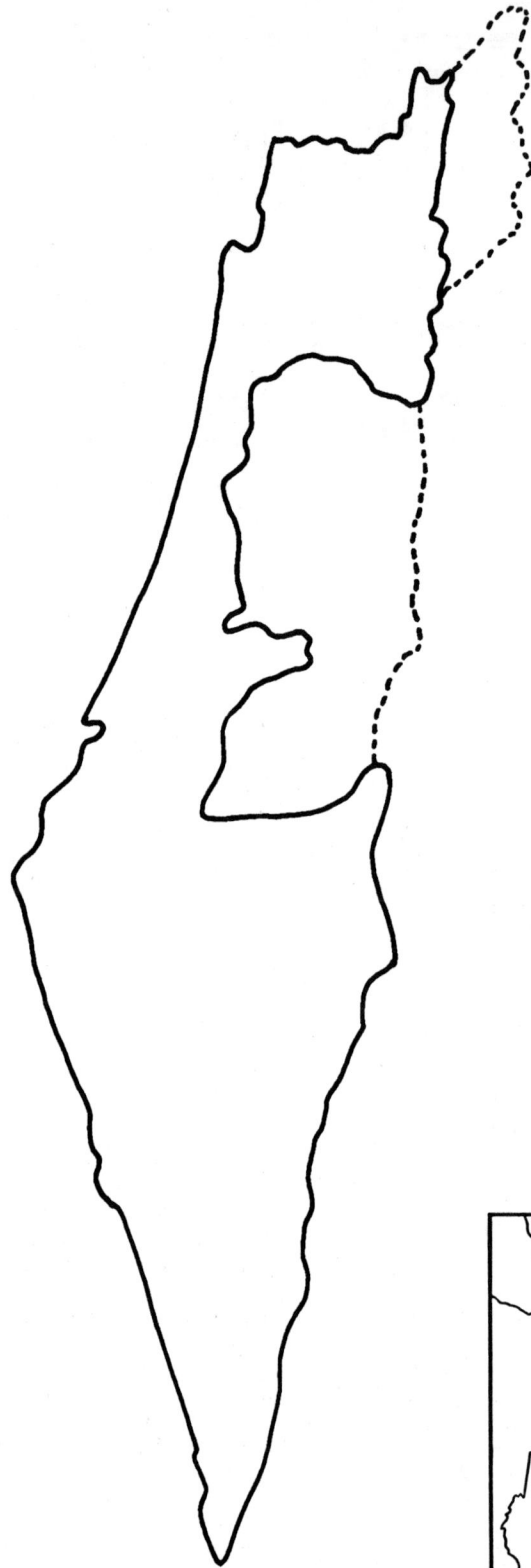

ISRAEL

ISRAEL

(IZ ray el)

Name _____

Date _____

DATE of INDEPENDENCE: May 14, 1948.

NATION'S CAPITAL CITY: Jerusalem.

OFFICIAL LANGUAGES: Hebrew and Arabic.

FORM of GOVERNMENT: Parliamentary Democracy.

AREA: 7,847 square miles (20,326 square kilometers).

POPULATION (est 1989): 4,371,000 people. _Density_: 557 people per square mile.
215 people per square kilometer.
86% urban (city) living and 14% rural (country) living.

LARGEST CITY: Jerusalem - 457,000 people.

ELEVATION: _Highest_: Mount Meron - 3,963 feet (1,208 m) above sea level.
Lowest: Dead Sea - 1,299 feet (396 m) below sea level.

ADDITIONAL INFORMATION: In Biblical times, the region was called _Palestine_. • Israel
was founded in 1948 as a home for Jews from all parts of the world. • The Arab
nations along Israel's borders strongly opposed the creation of Israel because they
wanted all of Palestine to be an Arab land. The Arabs invaded Israel the day after
it was established. However, the Israelis defeated the Arabs. Even today, Arabs
do not accept Israel, and are trying to destroy it. • Israel has one of the most
feared and powerful military forces in the world today, second only to the U.S.A.

Israel's Flag

Flag Description

1. The background of the flag is white,
   while the two stripes are dark blue.

2. The Star of David, an ancient
   Hebrew symbol, is in the center of
   the flag. It is the same blue as the
   stripes. The two colors are those of
   the **tallith**.

3. Color the flag the correct colors.

ISRAEL

Name _____

Date _____

EARLY HISTORY in BRIEF

The country of Israel is relatively young, only coming into existence on May 14, 1948. However, the region of Israel has one of the most fascinating, oldest and richest histories of all the countries of the world. The region was formerly named *Palestine*. It was the birthplace of two major world religions — **Judaism** and Christianity. It is referred to as the *Holy Land*, and is the sight of many events described throughout Bible and recorded in history. Followers of Islam, and the Moslem religion also consider Palestine as a **sacred** place. The Arab and **Hebrew** nations have fought over the control of the region for centuries. The fighting continues even today. (The word Jew has come to be used for all Hebrews. However, it comes from the name Judah, one of twelve early Israeli tribes.)

Prehistoric people lived in Palestine thousands of years ago, making it one of the world's first inhabited regions. The Amorites and Canaanites lived in the region about 3000 B.C. It was known as the *Land of Canaan*. It was about 1900 B.C. that the people called *Hebrews* (or *Israelites*) left Mesopotamia and settled in Canaan.

The Hebrews worshiped one God. The Canaanites worshiped many gods. This difference in their beliefs was the basis of many wars between the two peoples for hundreds of years. The constant warfare between the twelve tribes of Israel and the neighboring peoples led the Hebrews to unite under one king. Saul was their first king. King David replaced Saul. David established his capital in Jerusalem. Many of David's thoughts are recorded in the book of *Psalms* in the *Old Testament*. David's son, Solomon, succeeded him as King of the Hebrew nation. Solomon was the wisest and wealthiest of all men. The book of *Proverbs* in the *Old Testament*, which Soloman wrote, shows part of his wisdom. Solomon built a magnificent temple in Jerusalem for the worship of God.

In 721 B.C., the Assyrians from the region of today's Iraq, conquered the region of Israel. The Babylonians began to take control of the Palestine region after about 100 years. They finally conquered the region in 586 B.C. The Babylonians destroyed Solomon's Temple in Jerusalem. They also **enslaved** thousands of Jews and forced them to live in **exile** in Babylonia. Fifty years later, the Persians conquered Babylonia, including Palestine. Eventually, Alexander the Great conquered the Persian Empire, with Palestine as a part of the conquest.

Palestine became an independent Jewish state, called Judah, from about 145 to 63 B.C. It then was invaded by Roman troops and became part of the Roman Empire. The Romans called the region *Judea*. **Jesus Christ** was born of Jewish parents in the town of Bethlehem during the early years of Roman rule. By A.D. 135, the Romans had driven the Jews out of Jerusalem. The Romans then named the area *Palestine*, after *Palistia*. The Roman Empire controlled the region for the next 500 years.

ISRAEL

Name _____

Date _____

It was during the A.D. 600's that the Arabs conquered Palestine. They wanted to spread their newly adopted religion, Islam, throughout other parts of the world. Over time, many people in Palestine accepted their religion and other Arab customs and culture.

Christian crusaders from Europe wanted to gain control of the land where their religion had started. In 1096, the Crusades began. These Christians captured the city of Jerusalem in 1099, and controlled it for almost two hundred years. Moslems took control of Jerusalem in 1187.

In 1517, the Ottoman Turks took control of Palestine, making it part of the Ottoman Empire. The area had a small number of Jews and Christians living in the area. Most of the people living in the region were Arab Moslems.

By the 1800's, the Ottoman Empire was mostly controlled by various European nations. Jews began to move into Palestine and Jerusalem in order to live and die in the Holy Land. By the early 1900's, the Arab population in Palestine had grown rapidly. These Arabs opposed any Jewish settlement in Palestine. In 1920, Palestine became a territory of Britain.

During the 1930's, large numbers of Jewish people escaped Nazi **persecution** by moving to Palestine. (Millions, however, did not escape the cruel, brutal treatment and **slaughter** by Nazi Germany.) After World War II, thousands of Jews migrated to Palestine. On May 14, 1948, the Jews in Palestine proclaimed Israel an independent state. The next day, nearby Arab nations attacked Israel in an attempt to destroy the new Jewish state of Israel. Israel defeated the attacking forces. However, even today, there is much conflict in the region between Arab and Jewish nations.

A Palestinian family leaves their home with everything they could carry.

❑ ❑ ❑ ❑ ❑

ISRAEL

REVIEW QUESTIONS

Fill in each blank with the correct answer.

1. After the _____ drove the Jews out of the region, they named the
   area _____ .

2. Israel became a nation on _____ .

3. During World War II, Jewish people were _____ by _____
   _____ . Thousands of Jewish people _____ to
   _____ after _____ .

4. _____ and _____ nations have fought over the
   region for _____ .

5. _____ became an _____ Jewish state
   from 145 to 63 B.C.

6. The largest city, according to population, in Israel is _____ .

7. The capital city of Israel is _____ .

8. Israel is located by which body of water? _____

9. _____ was born in the town of _____
   in the early years of _____ rule.

10. Explain why Arab nations attacked Israel when it was first established as a nation.

    _____

Bonus ☆ ☆ ☆

Use another resource book and write a report on Judaism, the Holy Land, Canaanites, Hebrews, Mesopotamia, the *Book of Psalms* or *Proverbs* in the *Old Testament*, King Saul, King David, or King Solomon, Solomon's Temple, Babylonia, Alexander the Great, Jesus Christ, the Crusades, Jerusalem, Nazis or Adolf Hitler, or World War II.
See if you can also find current information about Israel in the newspaper.
Include pictures and maps in your report if they are applicable.

Jordan

Map • Facts • History & Review Questions

New Words to Learn:

Find the words in a dictionary and write the meanings on the lines.

1. **adopt** - _____

2. **crucify** - _____

3. **defense** - _____

4. **prophet** - _____

5. **Mohammed** - _____

6. **territory** - _____

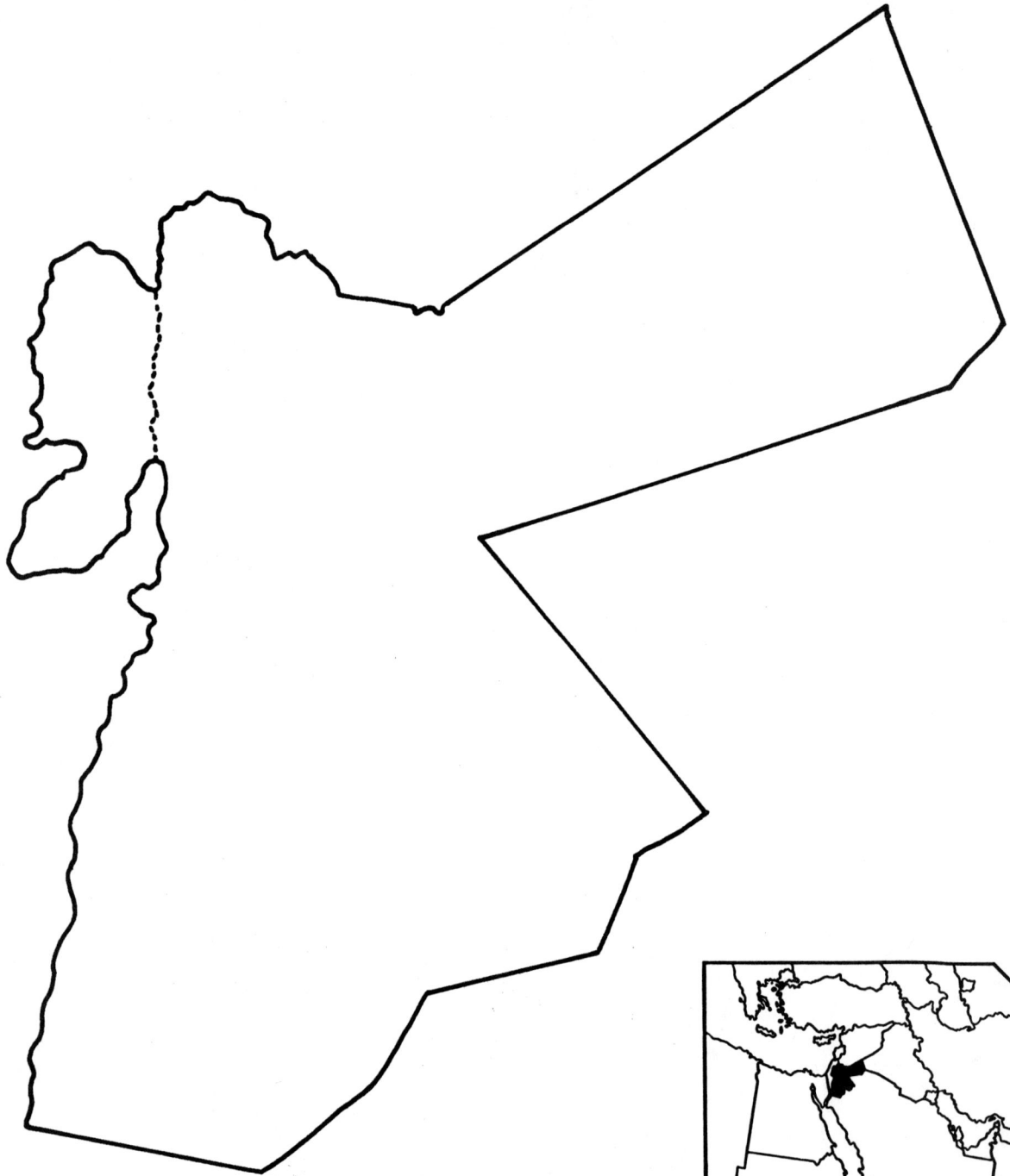

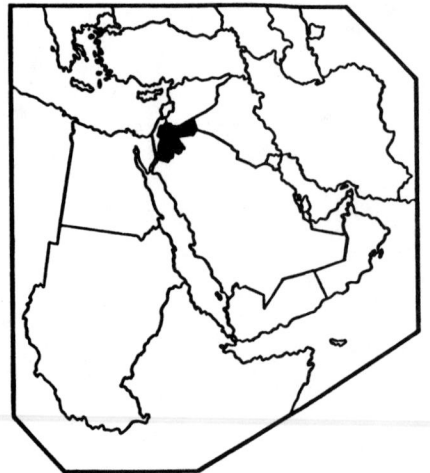

JORDAN

JORDAN
(JAWR duhn)

Name _____

Date _____

DATE of INDEPENDENCE: 1946.

NATION'S CAPITAL CITY: Amman.

OFFICIAL LANGUAGE: Arabic.

FORM of GOVERNMENT: **Democratic** Constitutional Monarchy.

AREA: 37,737 square miles (97,738 square kilometers).

POPULATION (est. 1989): 3,065,000 people.   _Density_: 81 people per square mile.
                                                                    31 people per square kilometer.
                            42% urban (city) living and 58% rural (country) living.

LARGEST CITY: Amman - 900,000 people.

ELEVATION: _Highest_: Jabal Ramm - 5,755 feet (1,754 m) above sea level.
                        Lowest: Dead Sea - 1,299 feet (396 m) below sea level.

ADDITIONAL INFORMATION: The River Jordan divides the country in two parts. One part in called the East Bank and the other is called the West Bank. Since the Arab-Israeli War of 1967, Israel has controlled the West Bank, where about 25% of Jordan's population lives. • Jordan was once called _Transjordan_ (meaning _beyond Jordan_) because it lay across the river from Palestine. The people who live on the East Bank are called _Transjordanians_. The people who live on the West Bank are called _Palestinians_. • About 90% of Jordan's people are Moslems, and 10% Christian.

Jordan's Flag

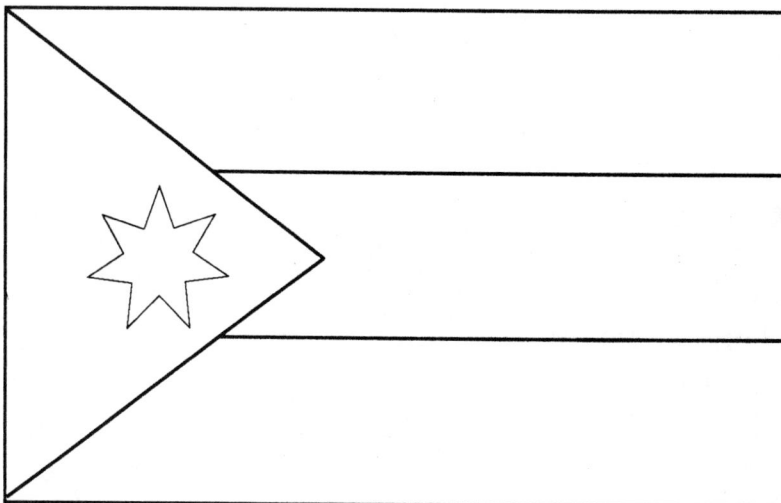

Flag Description

1. The top stripe is black; the bottom stripe is green; while the center stripe is white. (Several other Arab nations use the same colored stripes on their flags.)

2. The seven-pointed, white star on the red triangle background represents basic Islamic beliefs.

3. The flag's four colors represent four periods in Arab history.

4. Color the flag the correct colors.

JORDAN

Name _____

Date _____

EARLY HISTORY in BRIEF

People may have established one of the first settlements in the history of the world at the present-day location of Jerico. From 3000 to 1000 B.C., four small states developed east of the Jordan River. These four states make up the area of today's *East Bank*. The four states were Ammon, Edom, Gilead, and Moab. The two Hebrew states (tribes) of Judah and Israel developed on the west side of the river — today's *West Bank*.

During the region's early history, the Assyrians, Chaldeans, Egyptians and Persians all conquered and controlled the area of Jordan. Alexander the Great added it to his empire in 332 B.C. In 63 B.C., the Romans conquered Jordan.

After Jesus Christ was born and **crucified**, Christianity spread slowly throughout the region. In A.D. 313, the Roman Emperor Constantine converted to Christianity. This had a great influence in the spread of Christianity throughout the region of Jordan.

Moslem Arabs from Saudi Arabia conquered the Jordan region in A.D. 636. Moslems believed their **Prophet Mohammed** rose to heaven from Jerusalem. Therefore, the conquest of the region was very important to them. They considered Jerusalem a holy city, just as the Jewish and Christian people did. Over a period of time, the people in the region of Jordan **adopted** the Arab language and religion.

In 1920, after World War I, the region of Jordan became a British **territory**. A year later, Britain gave Jordan partial self-government. Britain named the territory Transjordan. In 1928, Transjordan became an independent state. However, Britain kept control of the state's **defenses**, finances and foreign affairs. It did not gain complete independence until 1946. In 1949, Transjordan changed its name to Jordan.

Crusaders during the Middle Ages tried to recapture Jerusalem from Moslem forces.

JORDAN

REVIEW QUESTIONS

Fill in each blank with the correct answer.

1. One of the first _____ in the history of the _____
   was established at _____ .

2. Who conquered the region in A.D. 636? _____

3. During the region's early history, which four peoples conquered and controlled the
   area of Jordan?   1. _____   3. _____

                           2. _____   4. _____

4. What year did Jordan gain its independence? _____

5. From what country did Jordan gain its independence? _____

6. What name did Britain give to the region? _____

7. Explain why the city of Jerusalem and the conquest of the region was so important to
   Moslem Arabs.

   _____

   _____

   _____

8. Explain what had a great influence in the spread of Christianity throughout the region
   of Jordan in the early part of this century.

   _____

   _____

   _____

Bonus ☆ ☆ ☆

    Use another resource book and write a report on Judaism, the Holy Land, Assyrians,
Chaldeans, Egyptians, Persians, Twelve Tribes of Israel (or one of the tribes),
the East and/or West Bank areas, or Jerusalem.
See if you can also find current information about Jordan in the newspaper.
Include pictures and maps in your report if they are applicable.

Kuwait

Map • Facts • History & Review Questions

New Words to Learn:

Find the words in a dictionary and write the meanings on the lines.

1. **deposit** - _____

2. **desert** - _____

3. **drought** - _____

4. **enterprise** - _____

5. **monopolize** - _____

6. **petroleum** - _____

7. **vast** - _____

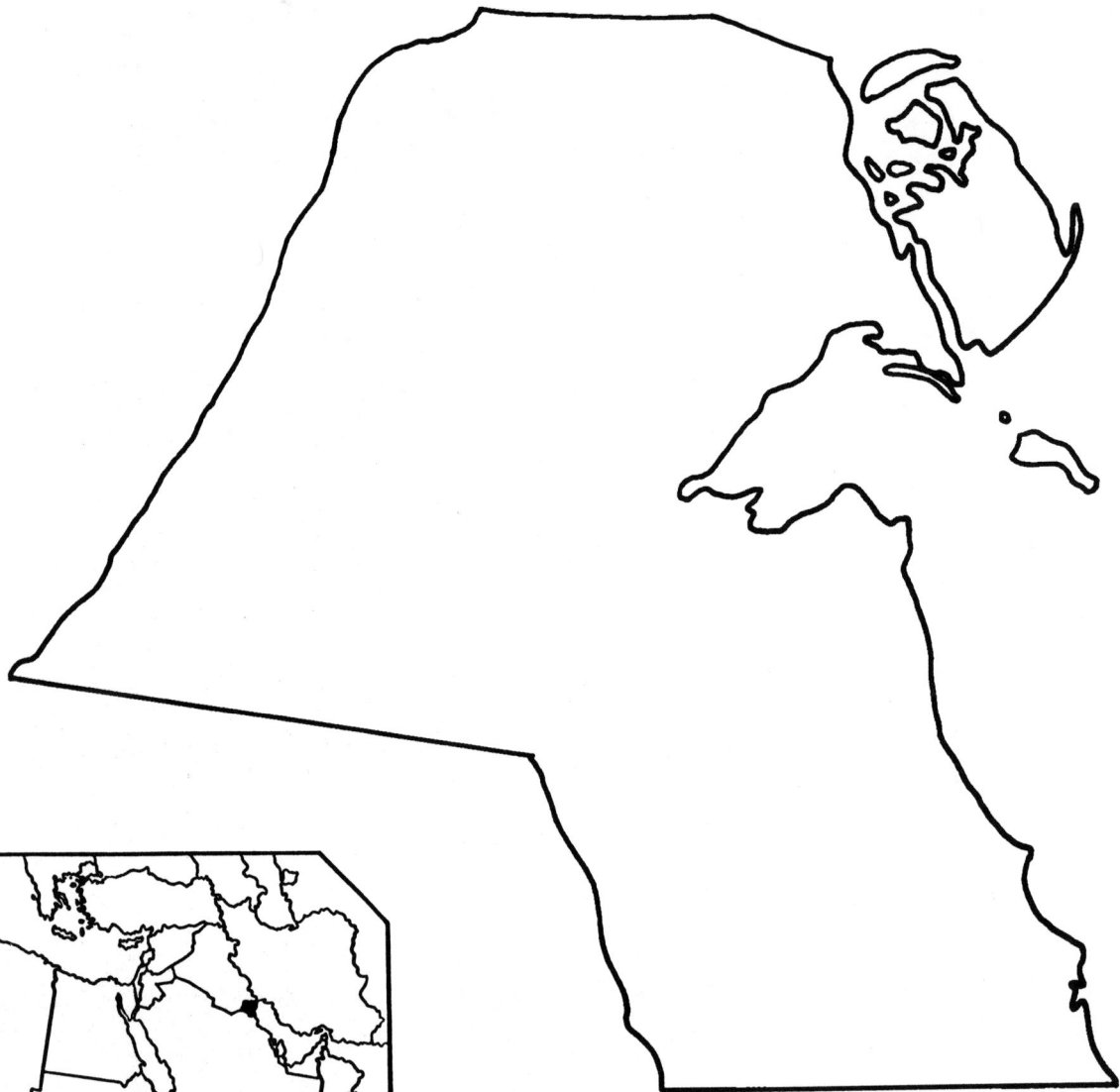

KUWAIT

KUWAIT
(koo WAYT)

DATE of INDEPENDENCE: 1961.

NATION'S CAPITAL CITY: Kuwait City.

OFFICIAL LANGUAGE: Arabic.

FORM of GOVERNMENT: Constitutional Monarchy.

AREA: 6,880 square miles (17,819 square kilometers).

POPULATION (est. 1988): 2,080,000 people.   _Density_: 302 people per square mile.
                                          117 people per square kilometer.
                          88% urban (city) living and 12% rural (country) living.

LARGEST CITY: Hawalli - 145,000 people

ELEVATION: _Highest_: Sea level.
              Lowest: Sea level.

ADDITIONAL INFORMATION: Kuwait is smaller in area than the state of New Jersey.
      However, it has over one-tenth of the entire world's known petroleum reserves.
      • Less than one half of the population is made up of Kuwaiti citizens. • Kuwait is
      one of the wealthiest of all nations in terms of national income per person. •
      Because of the heat, from May to October, business hours are from 7 A.M. to 1 P.M.
      and 4P.M. to 7 P.M. • Kuwait was invaded by Iraq in 1990, in an effort to take over
      its oil resources.

Kuwait's Flag

Flag Description

1. The top stripe is green; the bottom stripe is red; the center white. (Several other Arab nations use the same colors for the stripes on their flags.)

2. The vertical stripe (or polytagon) on the left is black.

3. The flag's four colors represent four periods in Arab history.

4. Color the flag the correct colors.

KUWAIT

Name _____

Date _____

EARLY HISTORY in BRIEF

Because Kuwait is mostly a **desert** land, there were few settled inhabitants before 1700. It was in 1710, when a small group of Arabs from the Anaiza tribe settled on the southern shore of Kuwait Bay. The finding of fresh water in the area allowed them to settle in the region. Historians believe that these people came from Arabia to escape a **drought**. They built a port that grew into the city of Kuwait.

In 1775, Britain made Kuwait the starting place for their mail service to Aleppo, Syria. British interest in Kuwait grew over the years. It became responsible for Kuwait's defense in 1899.

In the mid–1930's, Kuwait's ruler allowed an American–British **enterprise** to drill for oil. They discovered that there were **vast** oil **deposits** under the desert of Kuwait. After World War II, in 1946, Kuwait became a major **petroleum** exporting country. It soon changed from a very poor land to a very wealthy one — all because of its oil sales.

Kuwait became an independent nation in 1961. It then joined the Arab League, and in 1963, joined the United Nations. Over the years, Kuwait has given financial aid to several poorer Arab nations, as well as countries in Africa and Asia.

In July 1990, Iraqi troops attacked Kuwait. Iraq's leader wanted to gain control of the country and its oil. He wanted to **monopolize** the world's oil production. Iraq's leader, Suddam Hussaein, ordered his soldiers to murder Kuwait's people and destroy the country's buildings and resources. They set over 550 oil wells on fire, which burned millions of gallons of oil a day. Black smoke rose over the country for several months until the fires were put out.

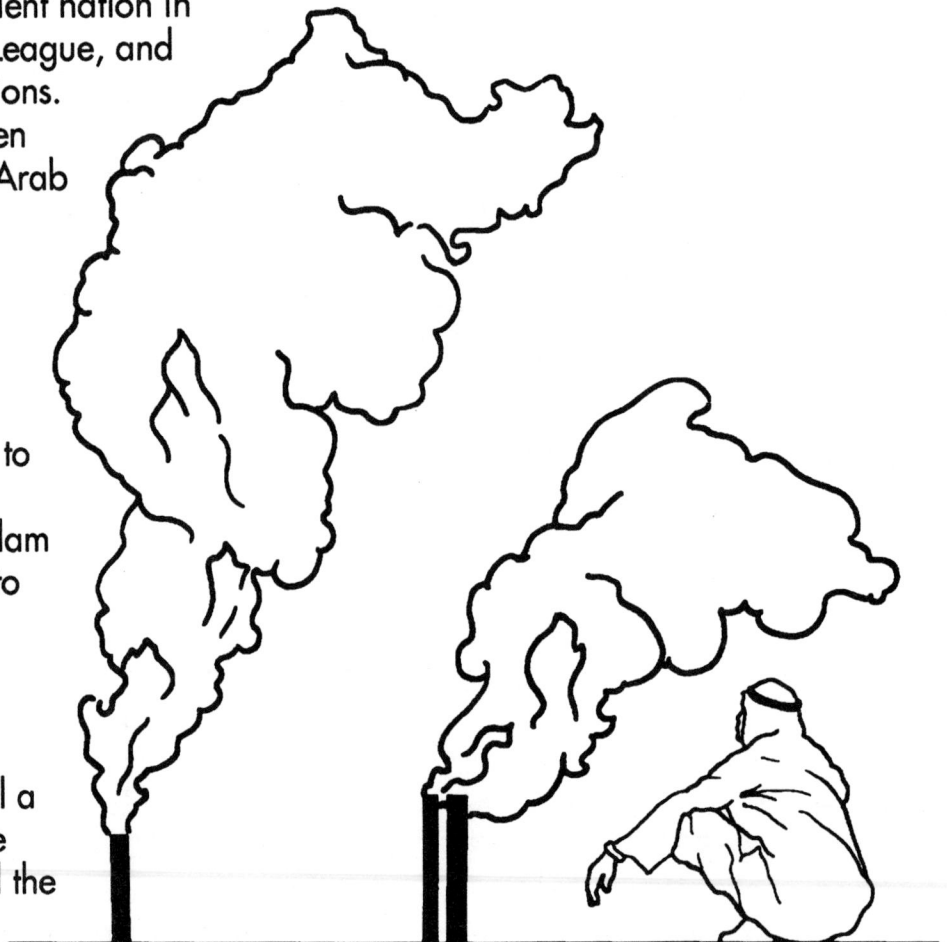

❏ ❏ ❏ ❏ ❏

A man watches the fires from burning oil wells.

KUWAIT

REVIEW QUESTIONS

Fill in each blank with the correct answer.

1. Pretend your country and city have just been attacked by a country several times bigger than yours, having a much more powerful military. Describe in detail how you would feel about the things that happened to your homeland and the help you received from larger countries that helped you fight the battles. (Hint: You might want to listen to the news or read old newspapers to find out some of the things Iraqi soldiers did to Kuwait, the people and country.) Use more paper if you need to.

_____

_____

_____

_____

_____

_____

_____

_____

_____

_____

_____

_____

_____

_____

_____

_____

Bonus ☆ ☆ ☆

Use another resource book and write a report on the war between Iraq and Kuwait in 1990-91. If you know somebody who fought in the war, interview that person and tell some of their experiences and thoughts about the war. Make sure you write who you interviewed and their relationship to you (even if only a friend of a friend). If you know anybody who protested the war, you can also write about him/her and the reasons behind their actions and beliefs. You can also interview both people and write their differences of opinions, and conclude which position you would take, and why. Include pictures and maps in your report if they are applicable.

Lebanon

Map • Facts • History
& Review Questions

New Words to Learn:

Find the words in a dictionary and write the meanings on the lines.

1. **affair** - _____

2. **coast** - _____

3. **culture** - _____

4. **peninsula** - _____

5. **prehistoric** - _____

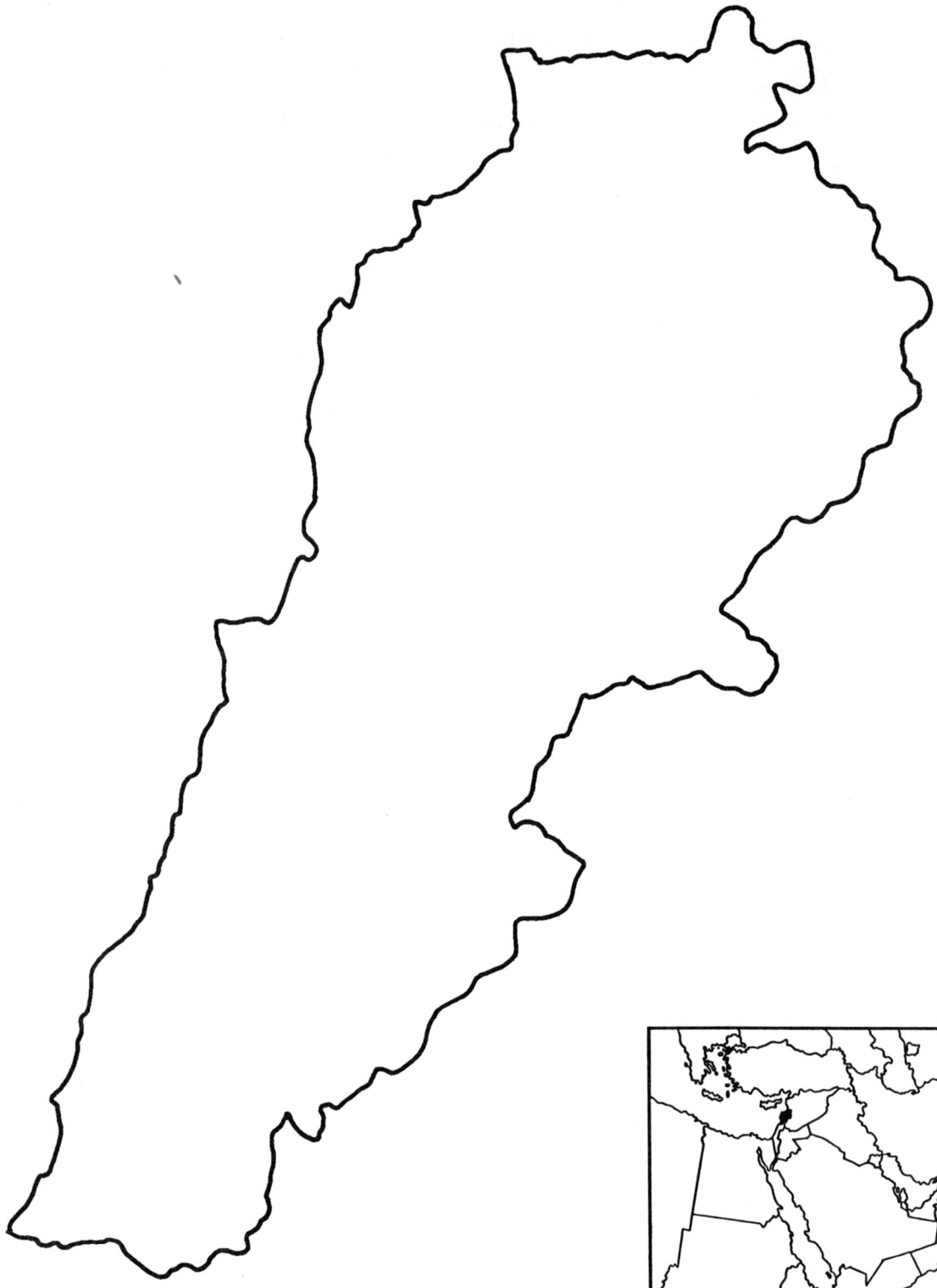

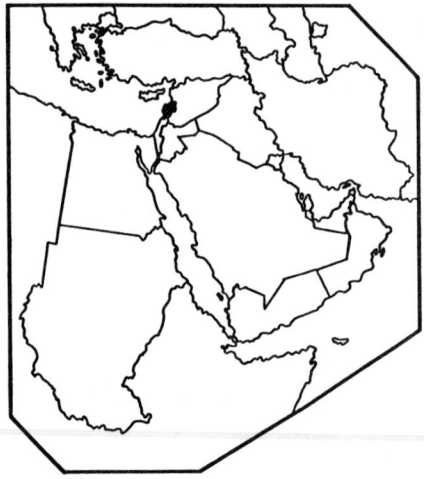

LEBANON

LEBANON

(LEB eh nen)

Name _____

Date _____

DATE of INDEPENDENCE: 1943.

NATION'S CAPITAL CITY: Beirut.

OFFICIAL LANGUAGE: Arabic.

FORM of GOVERNMENT: Republic.

AREA: 4,015 square miles (10,399 square kilometers).

POPULATION (est. 1989): 3,340,000 people. *Density*: 832 people per square mile.
321 people per square kilometer.
76% urban (city) living and 24% rural (country) living.

LARGEST CITY: Beirut - 1,500,000 people.

ELEVATION: *Highest*: Qurnat as Sawda - 10,115 feet (3,083 m) above sea level.
Lowest: Sea level.

ADDITIONAL INFORMATION: Lebanon has been the center of transportation, trade and
finance for many centuries. • Almost all of the people are Moslems or Christians.
• Political differences between the Lebanese Christians and Lebanese Moslems and
their Palestinian Liberation Organization (PLO) allies have led to several bloody
battles. • About 90% of the Lebanese people are Arabs. • Lebanese law does not
require children to attend school. However, most parents send their children to
both elementary and secondary school.

Lebanon's Flag

Flag Description

1. The top and bottom stripes are red,
   the center stripe is white.

2. The green and brown cedar tree on
   the center stripe symbolizes
   holiness, eternity, and peace.

3. Color the flag the correct colors.

LEBANON

Name _____

Date _____

EARLY HISTORY in BRIEF

The region of Lebanon has been inhabited since **prehistoric** times. The first well-known people to live in the area were the Phoenicians. They moved to the region about 3000 B.C. Their government and **culture** was well developed, establishing powerful independent city-states along the Mediterranean **coast**. The Phoenicians were very able sailors, traders and explorers. Out of a need to communicate with people from other nations, they developed the first **phonetic** alphabet.

From about 1800 B.C., foreign powers controlled the independent city-states that the Phoenicians had established. The other rulers of the area included the Egyptians, Hittites, Assyrians, Babylonians, and lastly, the Persians. In 332 B.C., Alexander the Great conquered the region of Lebanon. And in 64 B.C., the great Roman Empire took control of the region. Ruins of ancient Roman buildings and other structures still stand throughout the land. Some of the most famous of the ancient buildings are the temples at Baalbek.

Christianity was introduced to the people in the region about A.D. 332. Many of these Lebanese people became Christians. About 300 years later, Moslems from the Arabian **Peninsula** settled in the area. Islam gradually replaced Christianity as the main religion along the coastal areas. However, the people in the mountains remained strong in their Christian beliefs, customs and way of life.

The Ottoman Turks conquered Lebanon in 1516, and included the region as part of their empire. The capital of the empire was the city of Istanbul, located in today's Turkey. The Ottoman Empire ruled Lebanon until World War I (1914-1918), when France and Britain occupied the country. It was not until 1922 that France took control of Lebanon's political **affairs**. France united the Moslems and the Christians under one government. Lebanon became a totally independent country in 1948.

❑ ❑ ❑ ❑ ❑

Lebanon was one of seven Arab countries that first joined together to create the Arab League in 1945. The other six countries were Egypt, Iraq, Jordan, Saudi Arabia, Yemen, and Syria. The organization has since grown to a membership of 22 total Arab countries. The purpose of the Arab League is to promote cultural, economics, political, social and peaceful relations among its members.

Their flag has a green background with the Arab League's emblem in the center.

LEBANON

REVIEW QUESTIONS   Date _____

Circle each correct answer.

1. Lebanon became independent from ...
   a. France   b. Great Britain   c. Ottoman   d. Rome

2. Lebanon became totally independent in ...
   a. 1948   b. 1922   c. 1914   d. 1516

3. The first well-known people to settle in the region were the ...
   a. Phoenicians   b. Egyptians   c. Assyrians   d. Persians

Fill in each blank with the correct answer.

4. The capital of the Ottoman Empire was which city? _____

5. Lebanon is located along the coast of the _____ .

6. In what geographical area do most of the Lebanese Christains live? _____

7. In what geographical area do most of the Lebanese Moslems live? _____

8. The Phoenicians were very skilled _____ , _____ ,
   and _____ .

9. Explain how you think a religious belief, language and/or customs of a people can gradually change over a long period of time. (Use separate paper if you need to.)

   _____

   _____

   _____

   _____

   _____

   _____

Bonus ☆ ☆ ☆

Use another resource book and write a report on the Phoenicians, Egyptians, Hittites, Assyrians, Babylonians, Persians, Romans, Ottoman Turks, France, or Great Britain (or any of their empires), Islam, Christianity, or the Palestinian Liberation Organization (PLO). Include pictures and maps in your report if they are applicable.

Oman

Map • Facts • History
& Review Questions

New Words to Learn:

Find the words in a dictionary and write the meanings on the lines.

1. **breeder** - _____

2. **desolate** - _____

3. **heir** - _____

4. **horizontal** - _____

5. **inhabit** - _____

6. **immigrant** - _____

7. **immigrate** - _____

8. **sultan** - _____

9. **veil** - _____

OMAN

OMAN
(oh MAN)

Name _____

Date _____

DATE of INDEPENDENCE: mid-1800's.

NATION'S CAPITAL CITY: Muscat.

OFFICIAL LANGUAGE: Arabic.

FORM of GOVERNMENT: Republic.

AREA: 82,030 square miles (212,457 square kilometers).

POPULATION (est. 1989): 1,305,000 people.   _Density_: 16 people per square mile.
6 people per square kilometer.
7% urban (city) living and 93% rural (country) living.

LARGEST CITY: Muscat - 85,000 people.

ELEVATION: _Highest_: Jabal ash Sham - 9,957 feet (3,035 m) above sea level.
Lowest: Sea level along the coasts.

ADDITIONAL INFORMATION: Oman is one of the hottest countries in the world. Temperatures reach as high as 130°F. (54° C). • Most of the people are Arabs, poor and can not read or write. Most of them work on farms or in the petroleum industry. Some fish or work for cattle or camel **breeders**. • The people live in tents, or in houses made of mud and stone. • The women wear long, black dresses and **veils** that cover most of their faces. They wear the veil so no strange men can see their faces.

Oman's Flag

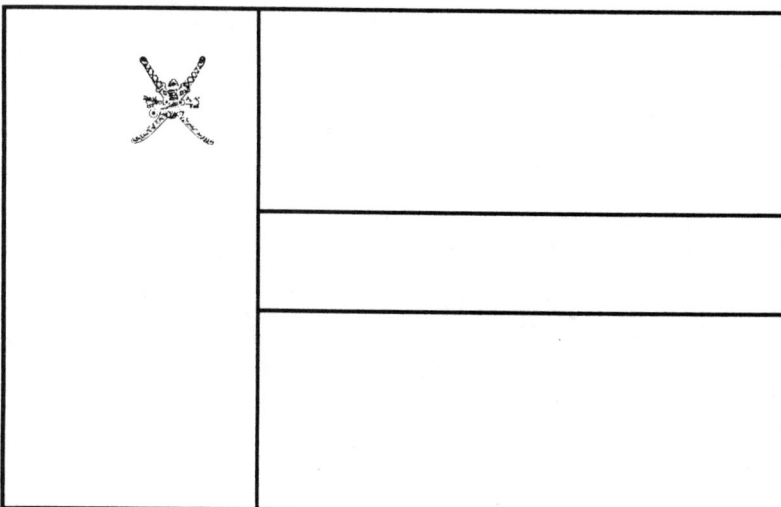

Flag Description

1. The vertical stripe on the left is red.

2. The **horizontal** stripes from the top to the bottom are white, red and green.

3. The national coat of arms is white and located in the upper left corner.

4. Color the flag the correct colors.

OMAN

EARLY HISTORY in BRIEF

Oman is a small country located on the southeastern tip of the Arabian Peninsula. Not much is known about the ancient people who inhabited the region. However, it is believed that Arab **immigrants** from the Arabian Peninsula were the first people to **inhabit** the area.

It wasn't until the early 1500's that the Portuguese took control of the region. Local Arabs forced the Portuguese out of the region of Oman in the mid-1600's. The present **sultan's** family came to power in 1743. The British have kept good relations with Oman since 1798, when they signed a treaty. In the 1800's, the **heirs** of today's sultan formed Oman as it is known today.

Oman is one of the hottest regions in the world. Temperatures sometimes get as high 130°F. (54 C). Within the country, there are only a handful of places that get over six inches of rain in an entire year. Most of the inland region of Oman is **desolate** land where nothing grows. The western border with Saudi Arabia has never really been officially agreed upon. Evidently, neither country is too concerned about it since the land is desolate and somewhat useless.

The country has very little in the way of manufactured goods. The country grows dates, limes, and pomegranates along the northern coast. Coconuts are grown along the southern coast. Oman has large deposits of petroleum. It is an important oil-producing nation.

❏ ❏ ❏ ❏ ❏

A Moslem man reads from the Koran, the Islamic holy book.

OMAN

REVIEW QUESTIONS

Circle each correct answer.

1. Portugal took control of Oman in ...

   a. prehistoric times   b. 1500's   c. 1743   d. mid-1600's

2. Oman is part of the ...

   a. Portuguese Empire   b. Arabian Family   c. Arabian Peninsula

3. Local Arabs force the Portuguese out of Oman in ...

   a. prehistoric times   b. 1500's   c. 1743   d. mid-1600's

Fill in each blank with the correct answer.

4. Today, Oman is a _____ form of government.

5. The official language of Oman is _____ .

6. The _____ border of Oman has never been _____ agreed upon with Saudi Arabia and Oman.

7. The capital city of Oman is _____ .

8. Oman is one of the _____ countries in the world. Sometimes, _____ get as _____ as 130° F. (54° C). In some places, it gets less than _____ of rainfall a _____ .

9. Oman gained its independence from _____ .

10. Why do you suppose the western border of the country has not been officially established?

_____

_____

_____

Bonus ☆ ☆ ☆

    Use another resource book and write a report on the Portuguese, Portugal, the Portuguese Empire, petroleum and/or the products made from petroleum. Include pictures and maps in your report if they are applicable.

Qatar

Map • Facts • History & Review Questions

New Words to Learn:

Find the words in a dictionary and write the meanings on the lines.

1. **emir** - _____

2. **deputy** - _____

3. **sect** - _____

4. **sheik** - _____

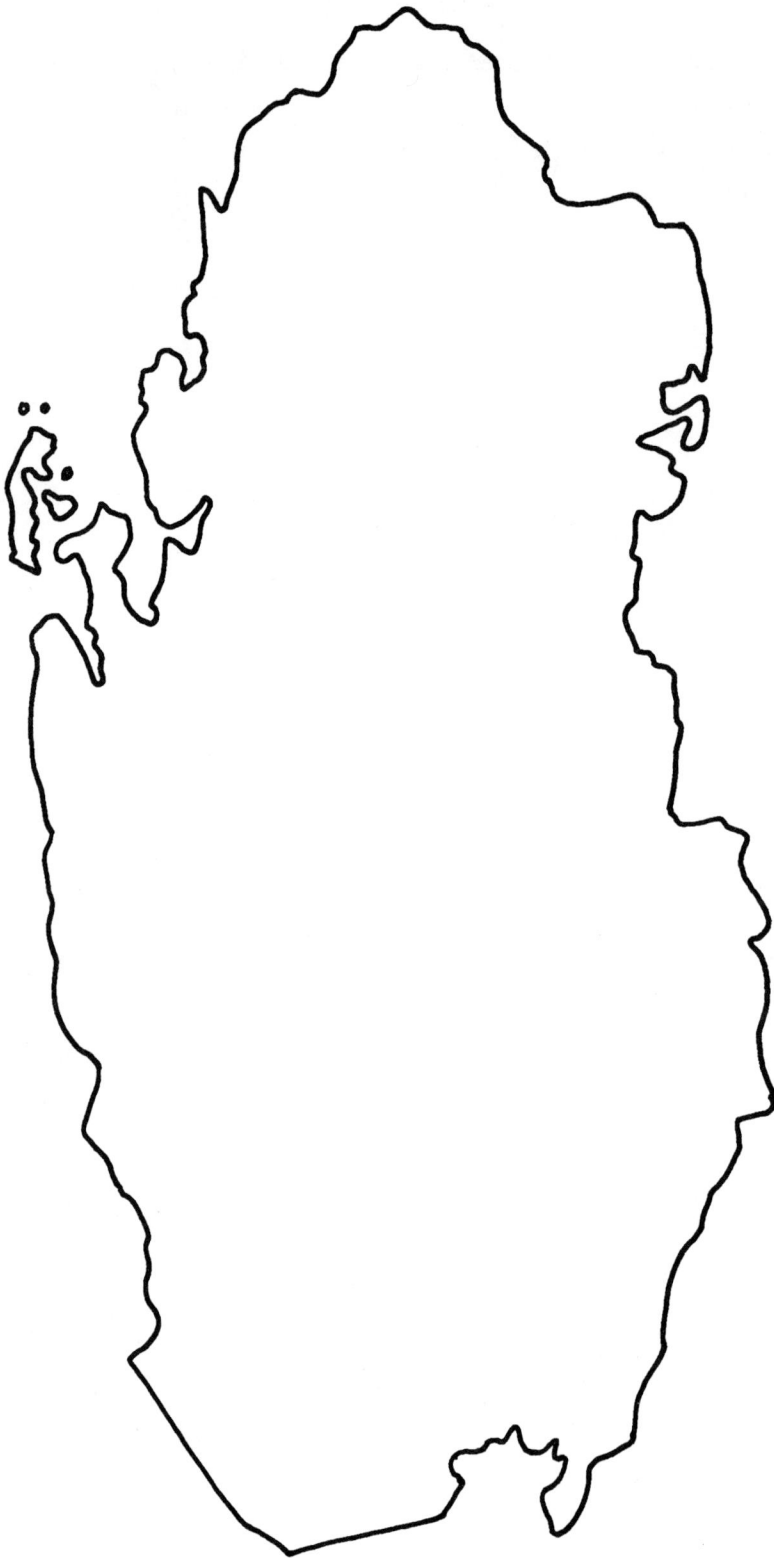

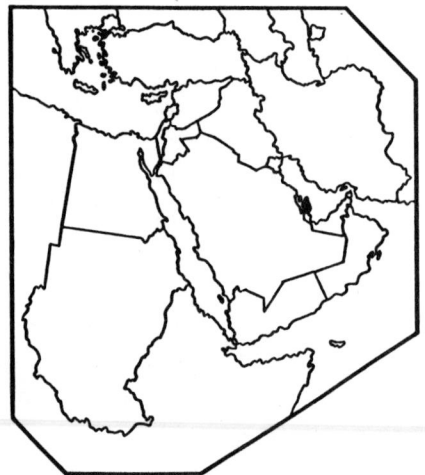

QATAR

QATAR
(KAY tahr or GAY tahr)

DATE of INDEPENDENCE: 1971.

NATION'S CAPITAL CITY: Doha.

OFFICIAL LANGUAGE: Arabic.

FORM of GOVERNMENT: Traditional Emirate.

AREA: 4,247 square miles (11,000 square kilometers).

POPULATION (est. 1989)**:** 498,000 people.   *Density:* 117 people per square mile.

45 people per square kilometer.

79% urban (city) living and 21% rural (country) living.

LARGEST CITY: Doha- 250,000 people.

ELEVATION: *Highest:* Orizaba - 18,701 feet (5,700 m) above sea level.
Lowest: near Mexicali - 33 feet (10m) below sea level.

ADDITIONAL INFORMATION: Most of the people live near Doha, the nation's capital and largest city. • Exporting of petroleum and petroleum products account for more than 95% of the country's income. • Qatar is a member of the *Organization of Petroleum Exporting Countries* (OPEC). • The government provides free elementary and high school to its children. The government also provides free health care for its citizens. • Summer temperatures sometimes rise over 120° F. (49° C).

Qatar's Flag

Flag Description

1. The left half of the flag is white.
2. The right half of the flag is maroon.
3. Color the flag the correct colors.

QATAR

Name _____

Date _____

EARLY HISTORY in BRIEF

Qatar is a small peninsula off the eastern border of Saudi Arabia. People have lived in the region for thousands of years. Today, oil is Qatar's most important product and main export. Before the discovery of oil in the region, the people made their living by raising camels, fishing or diving for pearls in the gulf and selling them.

The people living in the region of Qatar had no strong, central government until the late 1700's. This is when an Islamic **sect** from Saudi Arabia took control of the area. During the 1800's, **sheiks** of the al-Thani family became the leaders of the tribes living in Qatar. The region came under the control of the Ottoman Empire in the mid-1800's. In 1916, Qatar became a British protectorate during World War I (1914-1918).

It was in 1930 that exploration for oil began throughout Qatar.   Five years later, in 1935, the government of Qatar granted a 75 year drilling right to the Qatar Petroleum Company. Finally, in 1939, the company discovered oil in the western part of the country. However, World War II began that year and no further exploration took place until 1949. Since the early 1950's, oil production and sales has made Qatar a wealthy country.

Qatar became a totally independent nation in 1971. It then became a member of the Arab League and the United Nations. In 1972, the **deputy** ruler became **emir** after overthrowing his cousin.

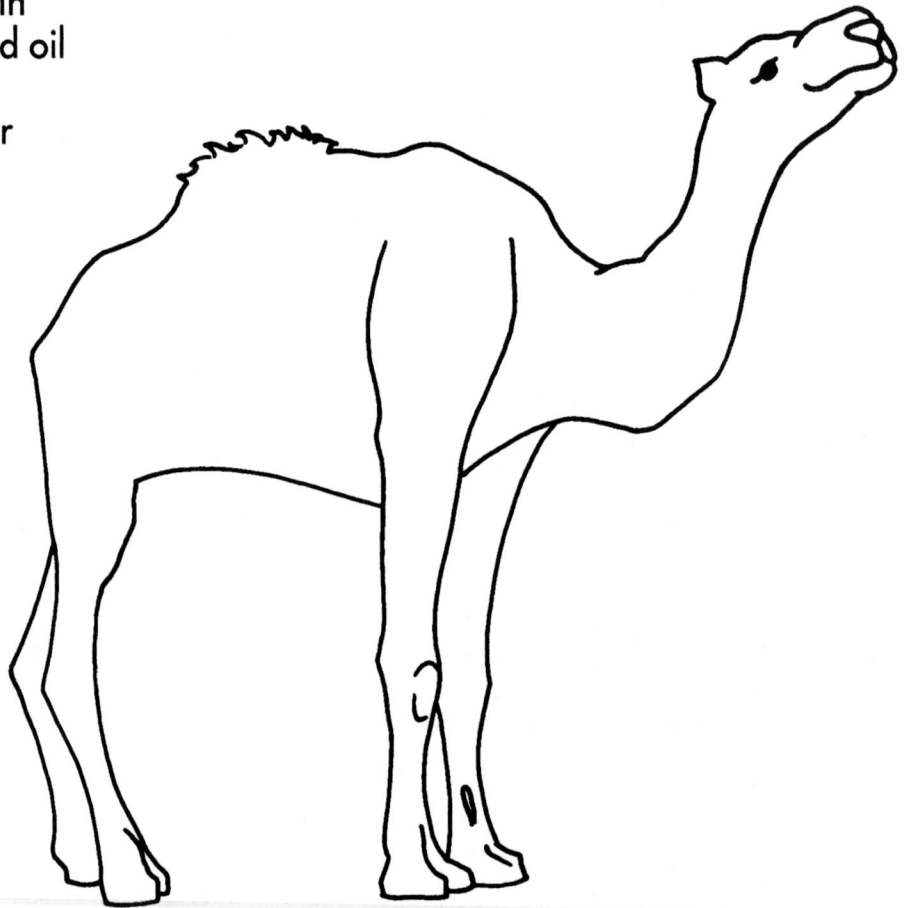

❑ ❑ ❑ ❑ ❑

Camels are used as the main transportation in desert areas.
They can go for days without water because of their ability to store it in their hump.

QATAR

Name _____

REVIEW QUESTIONS

Date _____

Circle each correct answer.

1. The ruler of Qatar is called ...

    a. king   b. pharaoh   c. emir   d. emperor

2. In what year did Qatar become totally independent?

    a. 1971   b. 1972   c. 1950   d. 1939

3. From which country did Qatar gain its independence?

    a. Britain   b. United Nations   c. Ottoman   d. Saudi Arabia

Fill in each blank with the correct answer.

4. The capital city of Qatar is _____ . According to _____ it is also Qatar's _____ city.

5. The current _____ of Qatar provides it citizens with _____ education, as well as free _____ .

6. What do the initials *OPEC* stand for? _____

_____

7. Today, _____ is the country's most important product and _____ export.

8. Explain why Qatar had to quit oil exploration in 1939.

_____

_____

9. Describe how the people of Qatar made their living before the discovery of oil.

_____

_____

Bonus ☆ ☆ ☆

Use another resource book and write a report on the Arab League, the United Nations, camels, pearls, OPEC, or petroleum and/or the products made from petroleum. Include pictures and maps in your report if they are applicable.

Saudi Arabia

Map • Facts • History & Review Questions

New Words to Learn:

Find the words in a dictionary and write the meanings on the lines.

1. **alliance** - _____

2. **Bedouin** - _____

3. **caravan** - _____

4. **civil** - _____

5. **dynasty** - _____

6. **feud** - _____

7. **inscription** - _____

8. **Semitic** - _____

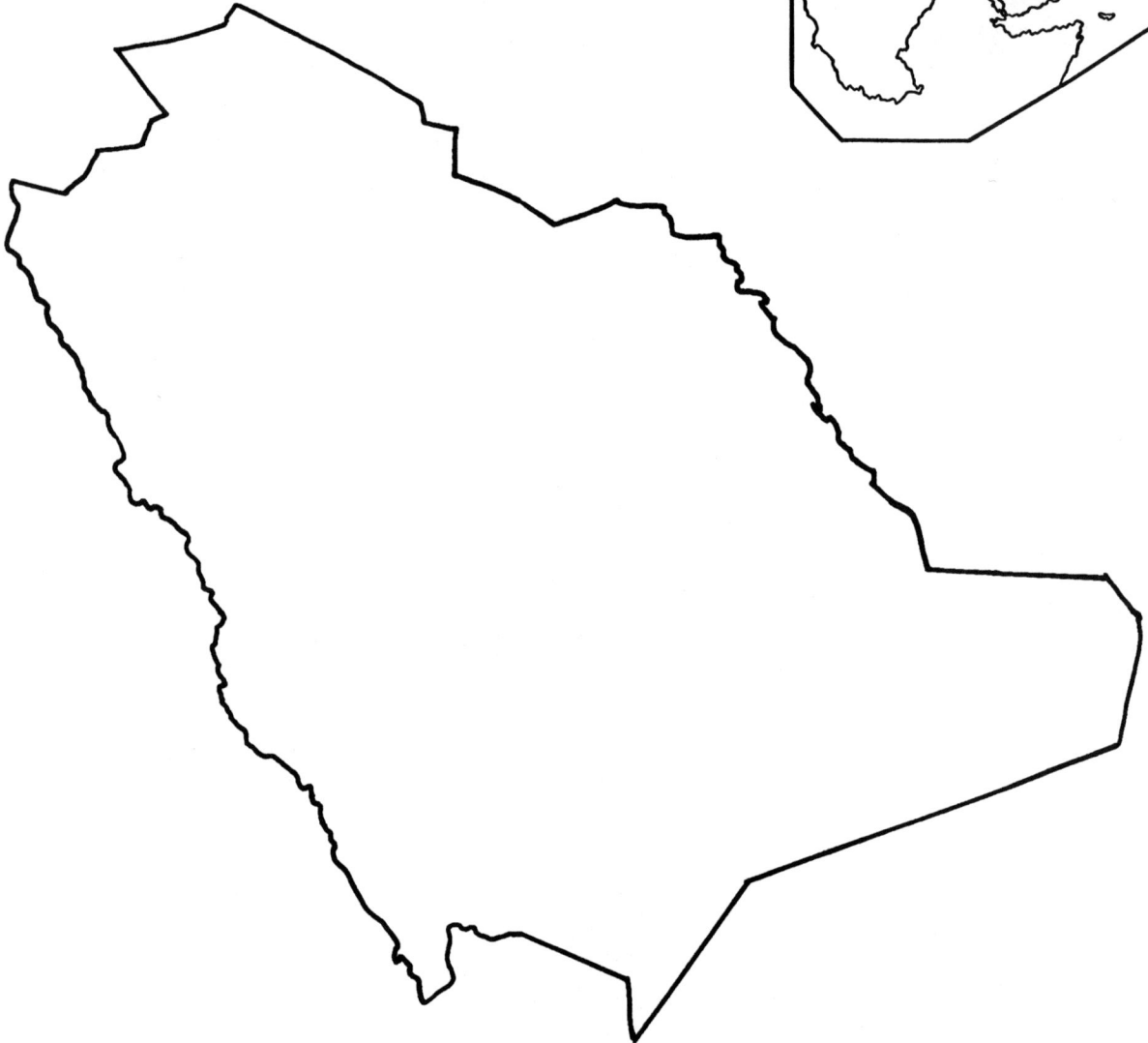

SAUDI ARABIA

SAUDI ARABIA

(SOW dee   uh RAY bee uh)

Name _____

Date _____

DATE of INDEPENDENCE: Proclaimed the Kingdom of Saudi Arabia in 1932.

NATION'S CAPITAL CITY: Riyadh.

OFFICIAL LANGUAGE: Arabic.

FORM of GOVERNMENT: Monarchy with Council of Ministers.

AREA: 839,996 square miles (2,175,580 square kilometers).

POPULATION (est. 1989): 3,500,000 people.   _Density_: 4 people per square mile.
2 people per square kilometer.
67% urban (city) living and 33% rural (country) living.

LARGEST CITY: Riyadh - 1,380,000 people.

ELEVATION: _Highest_: Jabal Sawda - 10,279 feet (3,133 m) above sea level.
Lowest: Sea level along the coast.

ADDITIONAL INFORMATION: Saudi Arabia includes most of the land region called the Arabian Peninsula. • Saudi Arabia is one of the largest oil producing nations in the world. It exports more oil than any other country. • It is a leading economic power in the Middle East. • Nearly all of the country's people are Arab Moslems. The two holiest cities, Mecca and Medina, of the Islam religion are located in Saudi Arabia. • Only about 20% of the people of Saudi Arabia can read and write. • The first public schools for boys were established in 1926.

Saudi Arabia's Flag

Flag Description

1. The background color is greenish-blue.

2. The sword is white.

3. The writing is a Moslem religious **inscription** written in Arabic.

4. Color the flag the correct colors.

SAUDI ARABIA

Name _____

Date _____

EARLY HISTORY in BRIEF

Thousands of years ago, various **Semitic** groups of people lived in the region known today as Saudi Arabia. **Bedouins** lived in the interior of the Arabian Peninsula. Trade centers were established along the **caravan** routes. These routes were important to the people living in the Arabian Peninsula because they linked the Arab people to other parts of the world.

People called the Sabaeans lived in the southwestern part of the region (including western Yemen) from about 700 B.C. The Sabaeans were very prosperous in trade. They were known for their fine spices, frankincense and myrrh. The Nabataeans controlled the trade routes in the northwestern part of Saudi Arabia and Jordan from about 350 B.C. to about A.D. 100.

Mohammed was the founder of the Islam religion. He was born in the city of Mecca about A.D. 570. Most of the people living in the region worshipped many different gods at this time. Mohammed believed in one god. Because many people opposed his beliefs in Mecca, in 622, he and his followers moved to Medina.

King Abdulaziz was the founder of the Kingdom of

SAUDI ARABIA

Name _____

Date _____

In 630, Muhammad returned to Mecca with an army and captured the city. He converted the people of Mecca to Islam. By the time of his death in 632, much of Arabia was under Moslem rule.

In the mid-600's, the Arabian Peninsula began to decline as the political and religious center of the Moslem Empire. In 750, the entire empire began to break up into small, individual states. During the next one thousand years, warring groups of people fought for control of different areas within the region.

During the early 1500's, the Ottoman Turks gained control over parts of western Arabia. In the 1800's, Britain established protectorates along the southern and eastern coasts of Arabia. However, the inland region remained under the control of the Arabian leaders.

During the mid–1400's, the Saud **dynasty** took control of a small area around the town of Dariyah. It was near today's city of Riyadh, in the central region. In the mid-1700's the Saudi ruler, Mohammed ibn Saud, formed an **alliance** with an Islamic religious reformer. This reformer wanted a stricter observance of Islamic teachings (Moslem laws) to be practiced by the Arabian people. With the support of the Saudi armies, the reform movement quickly spread throughout almost all of Arabia. The Saud dynasty enlarged the Saudi state by taking control of the areas that were converted in the religious reform movement. By the early 1800's, Mecca and Medina had been captured by the Saudi armies.

Soon after the fall of Mecca and Medina, the Ottoman governor ruling the nation of Egypt attacked the Saudi state to stop its expansion. By 1818, the Ottoman soldiers had taken control of most of the western coastal area along the Red Sea. They then marched into the Saudi capital of Dariyah and took control of that town. In 1824, the Saud family set up a new capital in the town of Riyadh. The Saud troops fought to regain their lost territory. By 1843, the Saudi armies had regained control of most of the land they had lost to the Ottoman troops.

After 1865, family **feuds** and **civil** war led to the weakening of Saudi power. By 1891, control of Arabia was divided between the few remaining Ottomans and various tribal chiefs throughout the region. The leaders of the Saud family went into exile in Kuwait.

In 1902, a young Saudi leader led troops from Kuwait and recaptured Riyadh. For the next 25 years the young Saudi leader, Ibn Saud, continued to regain the territory his ancestors had once ruled. In 1932, he proclaimed the union of the Kingdom of Saudi Arabia.

❏ ❏ ❏ ❏ ❏ ❏ ❏ ❏ ❏ ❏ ❏

SAUDI ARABIA

REVIEW QUESTIONS   Date _____

Circle each correct answer.

1. Who lived in the interior of the region?

    a. Semitic   b. Bedouins   c. Sabaeans   d. Mohammed

2. What year did Ibn Saud proclaim the union of Saudi Arabia?

    a. 1843   b. 1932   c. 1891   d. 1981

3. Almost all of the people are ...

    a. Christian   b. Moslem   c. Buddhist   d. Jewish

Fill in each blank with the correct answer.

4. The capital city of Saudi Arabia is _____ . According to _____ it is also Saudi Arabia's _____ city.

5. Saudi Arabia is one of the largest _____ of oil in the world. It _____ more oil than any other nation.

6. _____ is the official language of Saudi Arabia.

7. Explain why you think the caravan routes were so important to the ancient people of the region.

    _____

    _____

    _____

8. Explain how you think Saudi Arabia came to be called that name.

    _____

    _____

    _____

Bonus ☆ ☆ ☆

    Use another resource book and write a report on the Arab League, the United Nations, Mecca, Medina, Mohammed, Bedouins, the Sabaeans, OPEC, or petroleum and/or the products made from petroleum. Look in the newspaper and see if you can find current news. Include pictures and maps in your report if they are applicable.

Sudan

Map • Facts • History & Review Questions

New Words to Learn:

Find the words in a dictionary and write the meanings on the lines.

1. **continent** - _____

2. **expel** - _____

3. **mutiny** - _____

4. **nomad** - _____

5. **resent** - _____

6. **revolt** - _____

7. **scarce** - _____

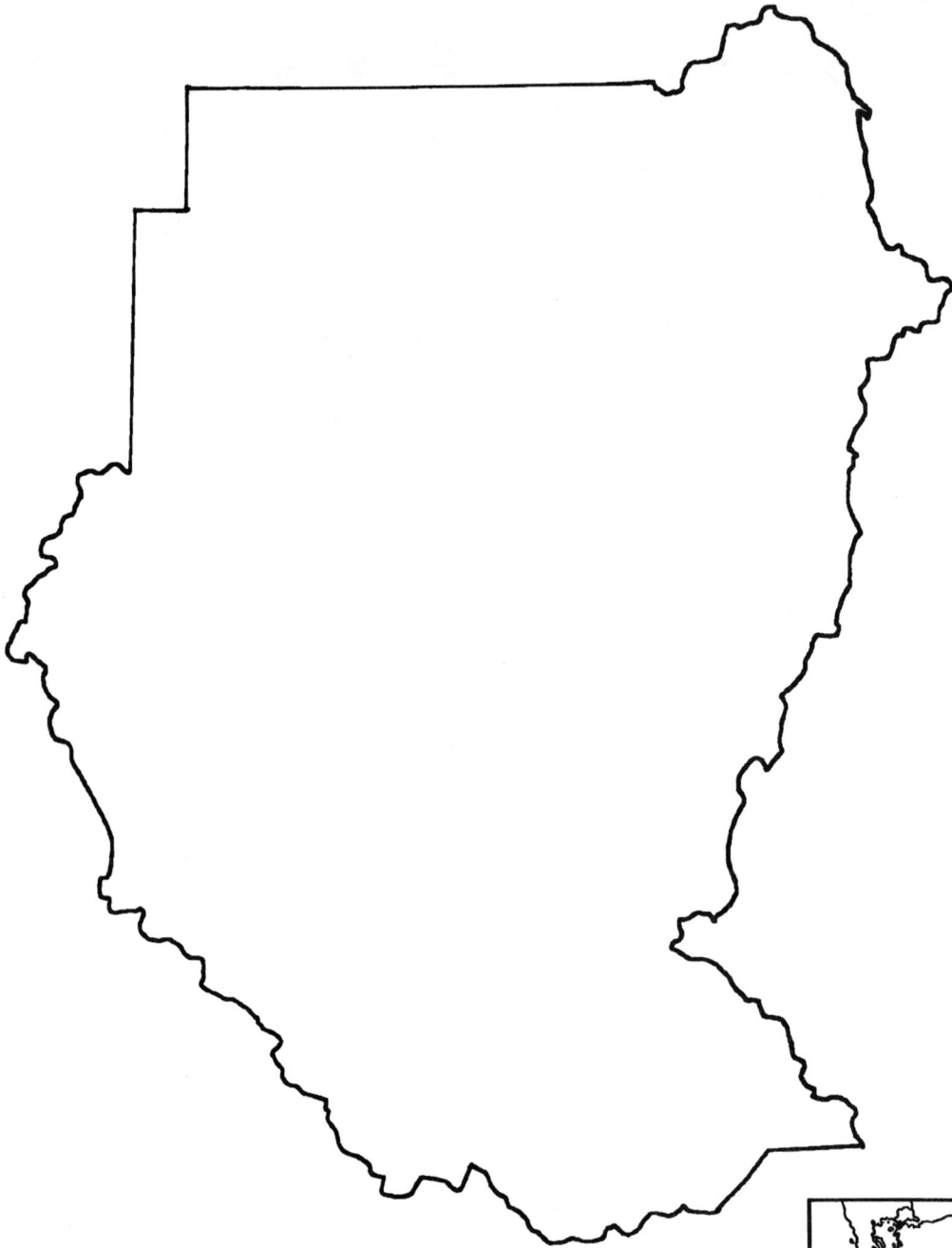

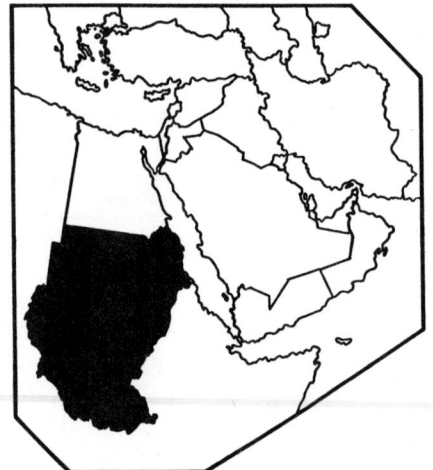

SUDAN

SUDAN
(soo DAN)

Name _____

Date _____

DATE of INDEPENDENCE: January 1, 1956.

NATION'S CAPITAL CITY: Khartoum.

OFFICIAL LANGUAGE: Arabic.

FORM of GOVERNMENT: Military.

AREA: 966,757 square miles (2,503,889 square kilometers)

POPULATION (est. 1989): 25,164,000 people. _Density_: 26 people per square mile.
10 people per square kilometer.
25% urban (city) living and 75% rural (country) living.

LARGEST CITY: Khartoum - 476,000 people.

ELEVATION: _Highest_: Mt. Kinyeti - 10,456 feet (3,187 m) above sea level.
Lowest: Sea level along the coast.

ADDITIONAL INFORMATION: According to area, Sudan is the largest country in the African continent. • Life centers around the water supply because it is so **scarce**. Most of the people live near the Nile River or one of its smaller river branches. Only **nomads** live in the desert in the northern part of the country. • Big game, including the rare rhinoceros, lions, leopards, elephants, buffalo, giraffe and other animals roam the forests and swamps in the southern portion of the country. • Less than half of the country's population can read and write.

Sudan's Flag

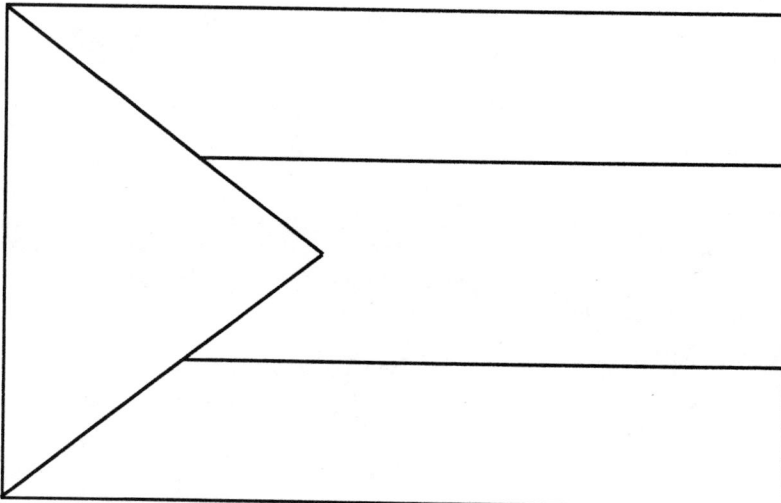

Flag Description

1. The top stripe is red; the bottom stripe is black; the center is white. (Several other Arab nations use the same colors for the stripes on their flags.)

2. The triangle is dark green.

3. The flag's four colors represent four periods in Arab history.

4. Color the flag the correct colors.

© GOLDEN EDUCATIONAL CENTER

SUDAN

Name _____

Date _____

EARLY HISTORY in BRIEF

After about 3000 B.C., Egypt invaded the northern region of today's Sudan many times. There was an important trading and cultural kingdom located in the northeastern part of the region from 1500 B.C. to about A.D. 350. The kingdom was called *Kush*.

There were several Christian kingdoms that were established in the area in the A.D. 500's. Moslem Arabs captured all of them between 1100 and 1600. It was in 1504 that the black-skinned Moslems called *Funj* established their capital at Sennar. Sennar is south of today's city of Wad Madani. The Funj captured and ruled much of the Sudan region. However, their power and influence declined in the 1700's. In 1821, Egypt conquered the Funj and took control of Sudan.

It was in 1881 that a Moslem leader declared himself leader and led a successful **revolt** against the Egyptians. His successor ruled Sudan until 1898, when British and Egyptian troops recaptured the region.

In 1899, Sudan was made a protectorate of Britain and Egypt. The British placed their people in most of the important governmental positions. Egyptians **resented** this and **mutinied** against the British. However, the mutiny failed and most of the Egyptian officials were **expelled** from Sudan.

After World War II (1939-1945), many of the educated Sudan people began demanding Sudan's independence. Sudan officially became an independent nation on January 1, 1956. It is the largest country, according to area, on the African **continent**. It is also a very poor country.

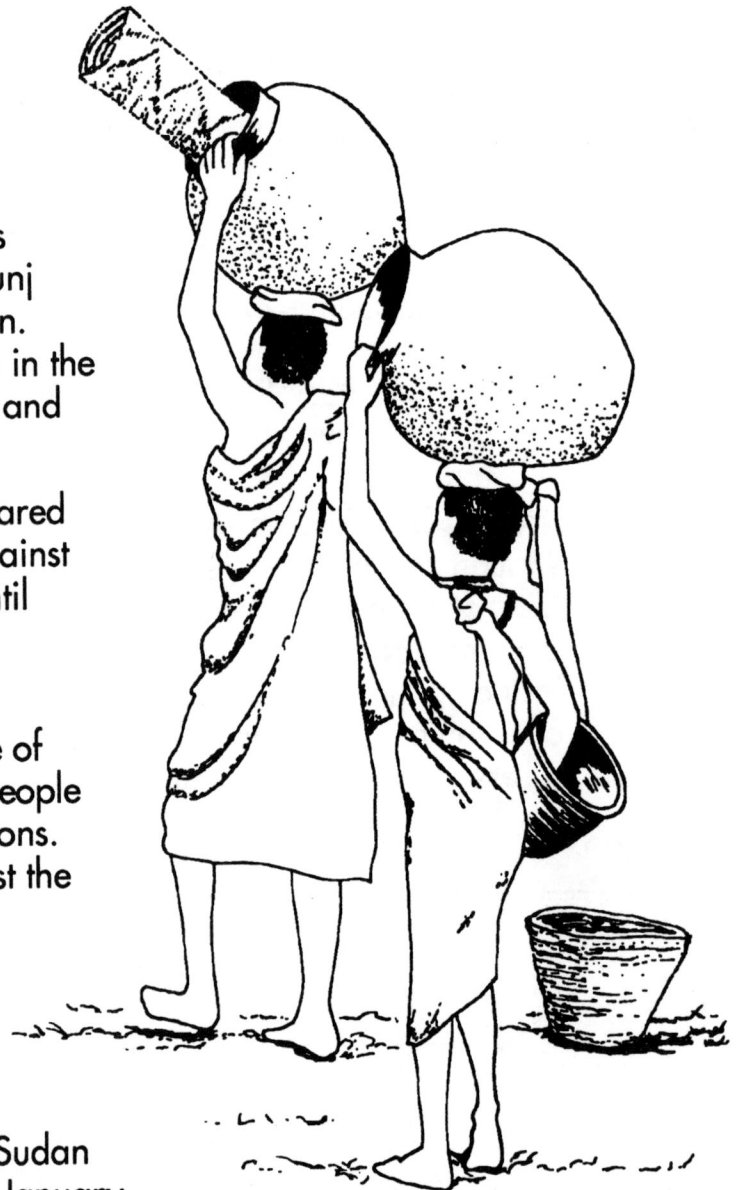

Two Sudanese women carry their purchases home from the market.

❑ ❑ ❑ ❑ ❑ ❑ ❑

SUDAN

REVIEW QUESTIONS   Date _____

Circle each correct answer.

1. Most of the people of Sudan live...

    a. by the Nile   b. in mansions   c. in the desert

2. Which was the capital city of the Funj?

    a. Wad Madani   b. Sennar   c. Khartoum   d. Kush

3. What year did Sudan gain its independence?

    a. 1945   b. 1899   c. 1898   d. 1956

Fill in each blank with the correct answer.

4. The capital city of Sudan is _____ .

5. _____ is the official language of Sudan.

6. What type of government rules Sudan? _____

7. From what country did Sudan gain its independence? _____

8. Why do you suppose only the educated people demanded Sudan's independence? Explain your reason in detail.

_____

_____

_____

_____

_____

_____

_____

Bonus ☆ ☆ ☆

    Use another resource book and write a report on the Nile River, the Kush Kingdom, the Funj, one or more of the animals living in the southern jungles of Sudan (see page 75 of this section), or the Egyptian or British Empires.
Look in the newspaper and see if you can find current news about Sudan.

Syria

Map • Facts • History & Review Questions

New Words to Learn:

Find the words in a dictionary and write the meanings on the lines.

1. **authority** - _____

2. **heritage** - _____

3. **scholar** - _____

4. **thrived** - _____

SYRIA

SYRIA

(SIHR ee uh)

Name _____

Date _____

DATE of INDEPENDENCE: 1948 (Gained complete independence).

NATION'S CAPITAL CITY: Damascus.

OFFICIAL LANGUAGE: Arabic.

FORM of GOVERNMENT: Republic.

AREA: 71,498 square miles (185,179 square kilometers).

POPULATION (est. 1989): 12,471,000 people.   _Density_: 174 people per square mile.
67 people per square kilometer.
50% urban (city) living and 50% rural (country) living.

LARGEST CITY: Damascus - 1,361,000 people.

ELEVATION: _Highest_: Mt Herman - 9,232 feet (2,814 m) above sea level.
Lowest: Sea level along the coast.

ADDITIONAL INFORMATION: The first known alphabet was developed in Syria in ancient times. • Syrian artists and **scholars** influenced the great cultures of ancient Greece and Rome. • Syrian cities of Damascus and Aleppo grew up along caravan routes and became world trade centers as early as 2000 B.C. • Moslems make up about 87% of the population. • Bread is the main food of the Syrian people. • As in most Islamic cultures, women in Syria have had very little freedom. They are often thought of as second class citizens by the male population.

Syria's Flag

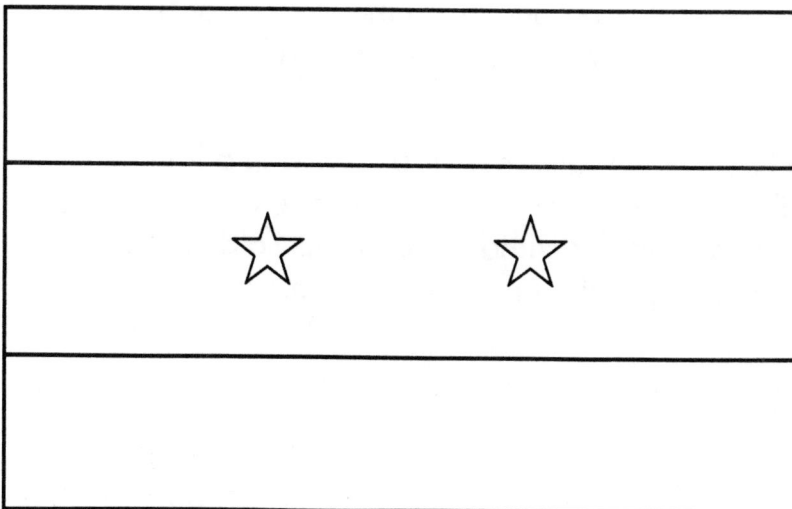

Flag Description

1. The top stripe is red; the bottom stripe is black; the center is white. (Several other Arab nations use the same colors for the stripes on their flags.)

2. The two stars in the white stripe are dark green.

3. The flag's four colors represent four periods in Arab history.

4. Color the flag the correct colors.

SYRIA

EARLY HISTORY in BRIEF

Syria is one the world's very ancient lands with a rich cultural **heritage**. Some of the oldest known civilizations grew up in the region of Syria. The world's first known alphabet was developed in Syria.

People were living in the area as early as 4500 B.C. However, historians are not sure as to which group these people belonged. They do know that the first Semites probably arrived in the area about 3500 B.C. The Semite people established independent city-states throughout the region. The Elba city-state in the northern area was a very powerful kingdom with a highly advanced civilization. It **thrived** in the area sometime between 2700 B.C. and 2200 B.C.

Several different Semitic groups ruled parts of Syria until 538 B.C. Some of these more well known ancient groups included the Akkadians, Arameans, Canaanites, Amorites, Hebrews, and Phoenicians. The Phoenicians settled along the Mediterranean Sea and became very skilled sailors. They carried Syrian culture throughout the Mediterranean world.

The Hebrews came to the region during the late 1200's B.C. They entered into the southern area of Syria. The Hebrew people introduced the belief in one God into the Syrian culture. In 732 B.C., the Assyrians conquered most of the region of Syria. They ruled the region for about 240 years until the Chaldeans took control.

In 538 B.C., the Persians conquered the Chaldeans and added Syria to their empire. Syria fell to Alexander the Great in 333 B.C., and the Romans in 64 B.C. Syrians lived under the Roman influence for almost 700 years. During this time, Christianity was born and developed in a part of *Greater Syria* called *Palestine*. It became the state religion in the A.D. 300's.

Moslems from the Arabian Peninsula invaded and conquered the leaders of Syria in 636. After many years, Islam replaced Christianity as the state's religion. Arabic gradually became the common language.

After World War I (1914-1918), the League of Nations divided Syria into four states: 1.) Syria, 2.) Lebanon, 3.) Palestine, and 4.) Transjordan. France was given the **authority** to manage the state's affairs. France finally withdrew all of its soldiers from Syria in 1946. Syria became a completely independent nation at that time.

❑　❑　❑　❑　❑　❑　❑　❑　❑　❑　❑

SYRIA

Name _____

REVIEW QUESTIONS   Date _____

Circle each correct answer.

1. Which year did Syria gain its independence?

    a. 538   b. 636   c. 1918   d. 1946

2. The official language of Syria is ...

    a. Arabic   b. Saudi   c. English   d. Hebrew

3. Hebrew people came to the region in ...

    a. 4500's B.C.   b. 3500's B.C.   c. 1200's B.C.   d. 732's B.C.

Fill in each blank with the correct answer.

4. The world's first known _____ was developed in Syria.

5. _____ is the largest city in Syria, according to population.

6. After World War II, the League of Nations divided the region of Syria into four states.

    List the four states.   1. _____   3. _____

                           2. _____   4. _____

7. Imagine you are living in Syria (in the area of Lebanon, Transjordan or Palestine) after World War I. One day you wake up and your country is no longer Syria, but one of the above countries. Explain how you feel and perhaps some of your actions.

   _____

   _____

   _____

   _____

Bonus ☆ ☆ ☆

Use another resource book and write a report on the Syrian alphabet, Semite peoples, Elba city-state/kingdom, Hebrew people, Christianity, Islam, or the League of Nations. You could also design and develop your own written alphabet with symbols you make up yourself.
Look in the newspaper and see if you can find current news about Syria.
Include pictures and maps in your report if they are applicable.

Turkey

Map • Facts • History & Review Questions

New Words to Learn:

Find the words in a dictionary and write the meanings on the lines.

1. **Armenia** - _____

2. **Anatolia** - _____

3. **barbarian** - _____

4. **Crusades** - _____

5. **disperse** - _____

6. **inevitable** - _____

7. **reform** - _____

8. **seize** - _____

9. **Thrace** - _____

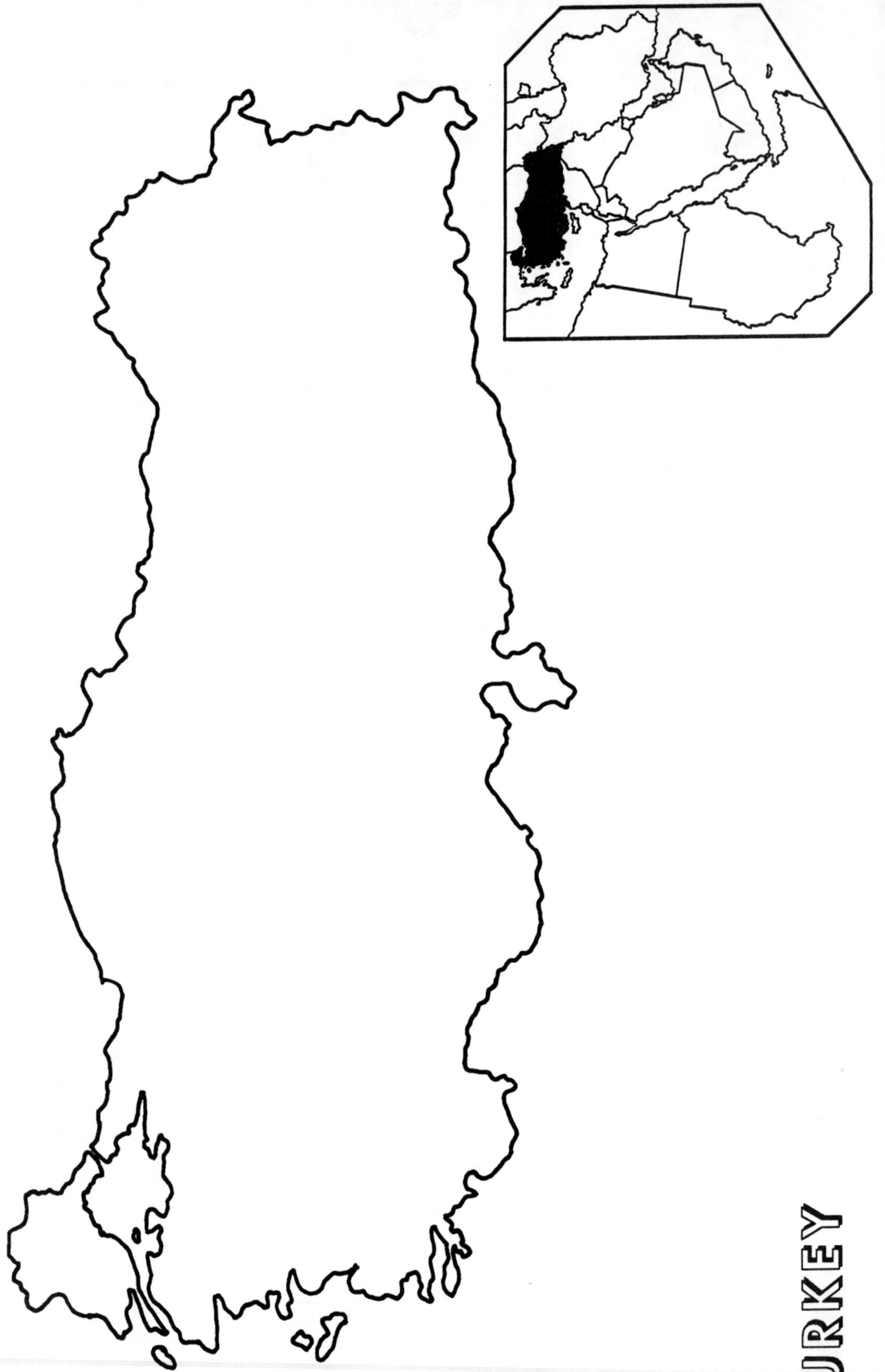

TURKEY

TURKEY

(tuhr KEE)

Name _____

Date _____

DATE of INDEPENDENCE: Became a Republic in 1922.

NATION'S CAPITAL CITY: Ankara.

OFFICIAL LANGUAGE: Turkish.

FORM of GOVERNMENT: Republic.

AREA: 301,381 square miles (780,573 square kilometers).

POPULATION (est. 1989): 56,549,000 people.   _Density_: 188 people per square mile.
                                                                                72 people per square kilometer.
                                          44% urban (city) living and 56% rural (country) living.

LARGEST CITY: Istanbul - 5,800,000 people.

ELEVATION: _Highest_: Mt. Ararat - 17,011 feet (5,185 m) above sea level.
                      Lowest: Sea level along the coast.

ADDITIONAL INFORMATION: About 90% of Turkey's population are descendants of an
      Asian people called _Turks_. • One part of Turkey, Anatolia, is located in the
      continent of Asia; and another part of the country, Thrace, is on the continent of
      Europe. • The current city of Istanbul was first named _Byzantium_ and then
      renamed _Constantinople_. • Islamic law strongly influenced Turkish lifestyle for
      nearly 1000 years. However, **reforms** in the 1920's outlawed many Islamic
      practices. Even today some people accept the changes, while others do not.

Turkey's Flag

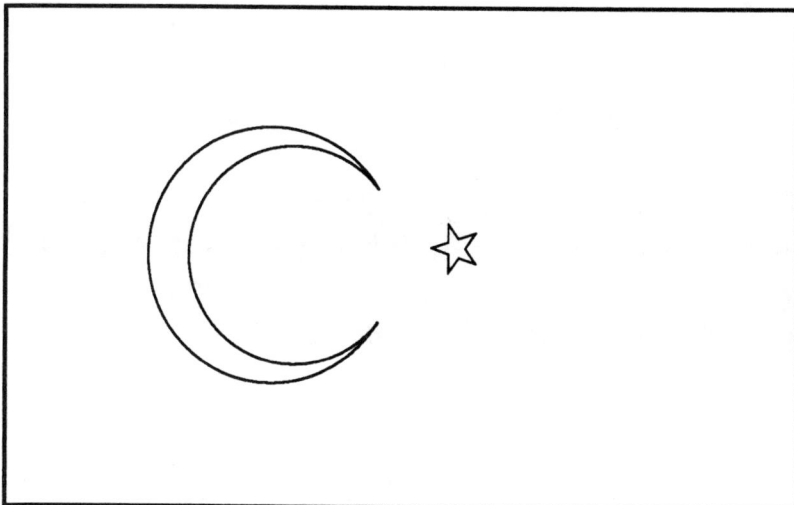

Flag Description

1. The background is red.

2. The crescent and five pointed star are white.

3. These are traditional symbols used in the Islamic religion.

4. Color the flag the correct colors.

TURKEY

Name _____

Date _____

EARLY HISTORY in BRIEF

The earliest known people to live in the region known today as Turkey were the Hittites. It was about 2000 B.C. when they began to migrate from central Asia into the region. During the next several years, they conquered and ruled most of **Anatolia** and parts of Mesopotamia and Syria. By 1500 B.C., the Hittites had built a powerful empire. They were the leading rulers of the entire Middle East region.

From 1200 to 500 B.C., areas of Anatolia were conquered by the Phrygians, the Lydians and other peoples. The Greeks established several city-states along the Aegean coast. It was in about 500 B.C. that the Persian Empire **seized** control of Anatolia and **Thrace**. Alexander the Great crushed the Persian forces in 331 B.C. to gain control of the regions. In 63 B.C. the regions fell to Roman conquest. Anatolia was at peace under Roman rule for nearly 400 years.

In A.D. 330, the Roman emperor Constantine the Great moved the capital of his empire. He moved it from Rome to the ancient town of Byzantium located in Thrace. He renamed Byzantium *Constantinople*, which means *city of Constantine*. In 395, the Roman Empire split into two parts — the East Roman Empire ,which included Anatolia and Thrace, and the West Roman Empire. In the mid-400's, the West Roman Empire was conquered by **barbarians**. The East Roman Empire, also called the *Byzantine Empire*, continued to thrive. Byzantine emperors ruled all of what is now Turkey until the late 1000's.

The Seljuk Turks became one of the first Turkic peoples to rule in Turkey. The Seljuks were Moslems from the south-central area of Russia and northern Mongolia. During the mid-1000's they conquered **Armenia**, the Holy Land (Palestine) and most of Iran. It was in 1071 that the Seljuks destroyed most of the Byzantine armies in Anatolia. They set up an empire with Iconium (today's Konya) as their capital. The Greek language and Christianity were gradually replaced in Anatolia by the Turkish language and the Islam religion.

During the **Crusades,** the Turks were driven out of Palestine and western Anatolia. The Seljuk empire remained in the rest of the region until 1243, when the Asian people known as the Mongols completely defeated them.

In the 1300's, a group of Turks called the Ottomans began to build a large and very powerful empire. By the late 1300's, they had gained control of the western two-thirds of Anatolia, all of Greece, and most of Thrace. All that remained of the Byzantine Empire was the area around Constantinople. In 1453, Ottoman soldiers conquered Constantinople, ending the Byzantine Empire.

TURKEY

Name _____

Date _____

By 1481, the Ottoman Empire reached from the Danube River in Europe to southern Anatolia. The Ottoman Empire reached its peak in the 1500's. It had extended its holdings from Europe, to northern Africa, to Yemen on the Arabian Peninsula, and to Persia. It became the leading naval power in the Mediterranean Sea.

During the 1700's, the Ottoman Empire steadily weakened. In 1774, the Turks lost a six-year war with Russia and were forced to allow Russian ships through the Straits (the Turkish waters that link the Black Sea to the Mediterranean Sea).

The Ottoman Empire came to be called the *Sick Man of Europe*. It continued to lose territory during the 1800's and declining in power. It was called the *Sick Man of Europe* because it was not progressing and the fall was **inevitable**. The Ottoman leaders tried to stop the decline of the empire by reorganizing the military and improving the educational system. In 1876, Turkey adopted its first constitution.

Turkey entered World War I (1914–1918) on the side of Germany and Austria-Hungary in an attempt to regain its lost territory. However, they lost the war, and what was left of the Ottoman Empire was **dispersed**.

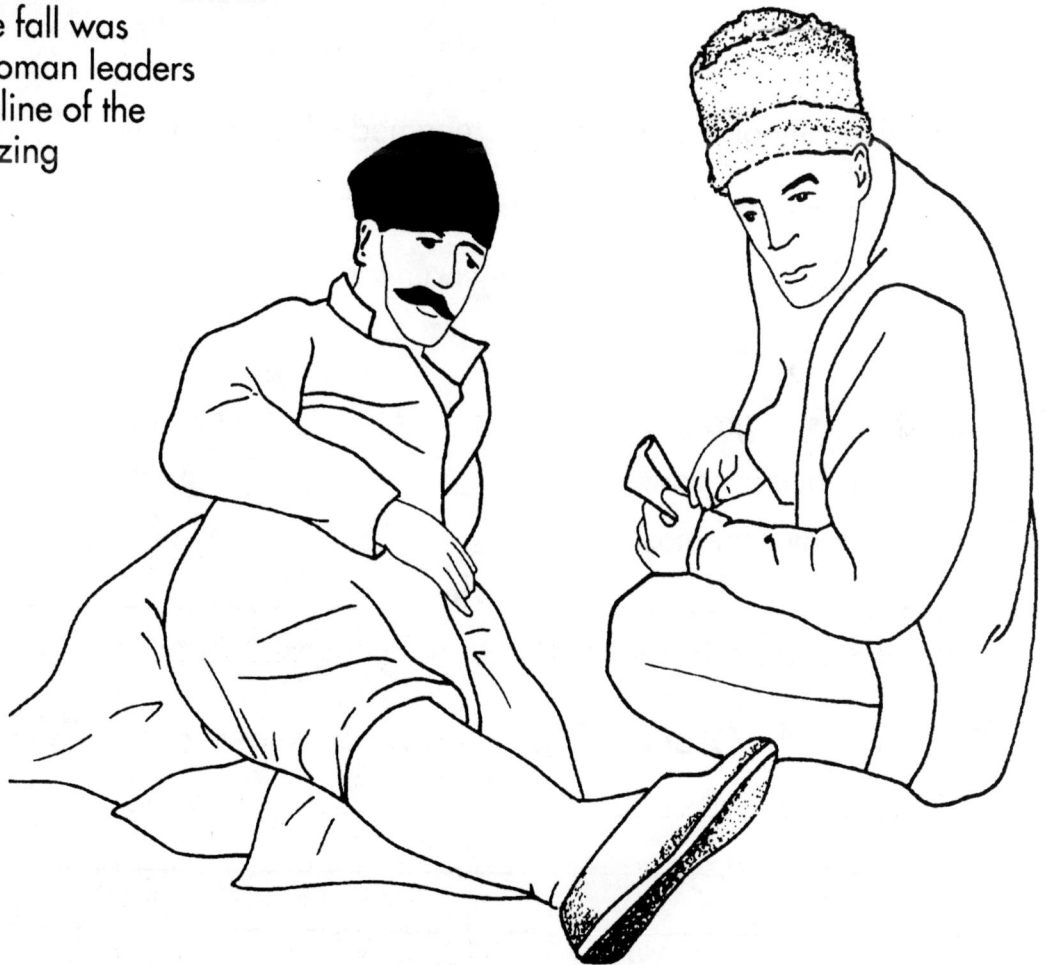

❏   ❏   ❏

Two young Turkish men relax on some sacks.

TURKEY

REVIEW QUESTIONS

Circle each correct answer.

1. When did Turkey adopt its first constitution?

   a. 1876   b. 1700   c. 1774   d. 1453

2. The official language of Turkey is ...

   a. Asian   b. Arabic   c. Turkish   d. Ottoman

3. What was the name of the Turkish Empire?

   a. Byzantine   b. Arabic   c. Turkish   d. Ottoman

Fill in each blank with the correct answer.

4. The capital city of Turkey is _____ . According to population, _____ is the largest city.

5. The ancient city of Byzantium was renamed what two names?

   1. _____   2. _____

6. What are the two regions of Turkey named?

   1. _____   2. _____

7. In the 1300's, a group of _____ called the _____ began to build a powerful _____ . By late in that century, they had gained control of most of _____ , all of _____ , and most of _____ . The _____ reached its peak in the 1500's.

8. Explain why the Ottoman Empire came to be known as the *Sick Man of Europe.*

   _____

   _____

   _____

Bonus ☆ ☆ ☆

Use another resource book and write a report on ancient Greece or Rome, Armenia, the Persian Empire, the Crusades, the Turkish and Russian six year war, or World War I. Look in the newspaper and see if you can find current news about Turkey. Include pictures and maps in your report if they are applicable.

United Arab Emirates

Map • Facts • History & Review Questions

New Words to Learn:

Find the words in a dictionary and write the meanings on the lines.

1. **compete** - _____

2. **internal** - _____

3. **nomads** - _____

4. **strategic** - _____

5. **thatch** - _____

6. **Trucial States** - _____

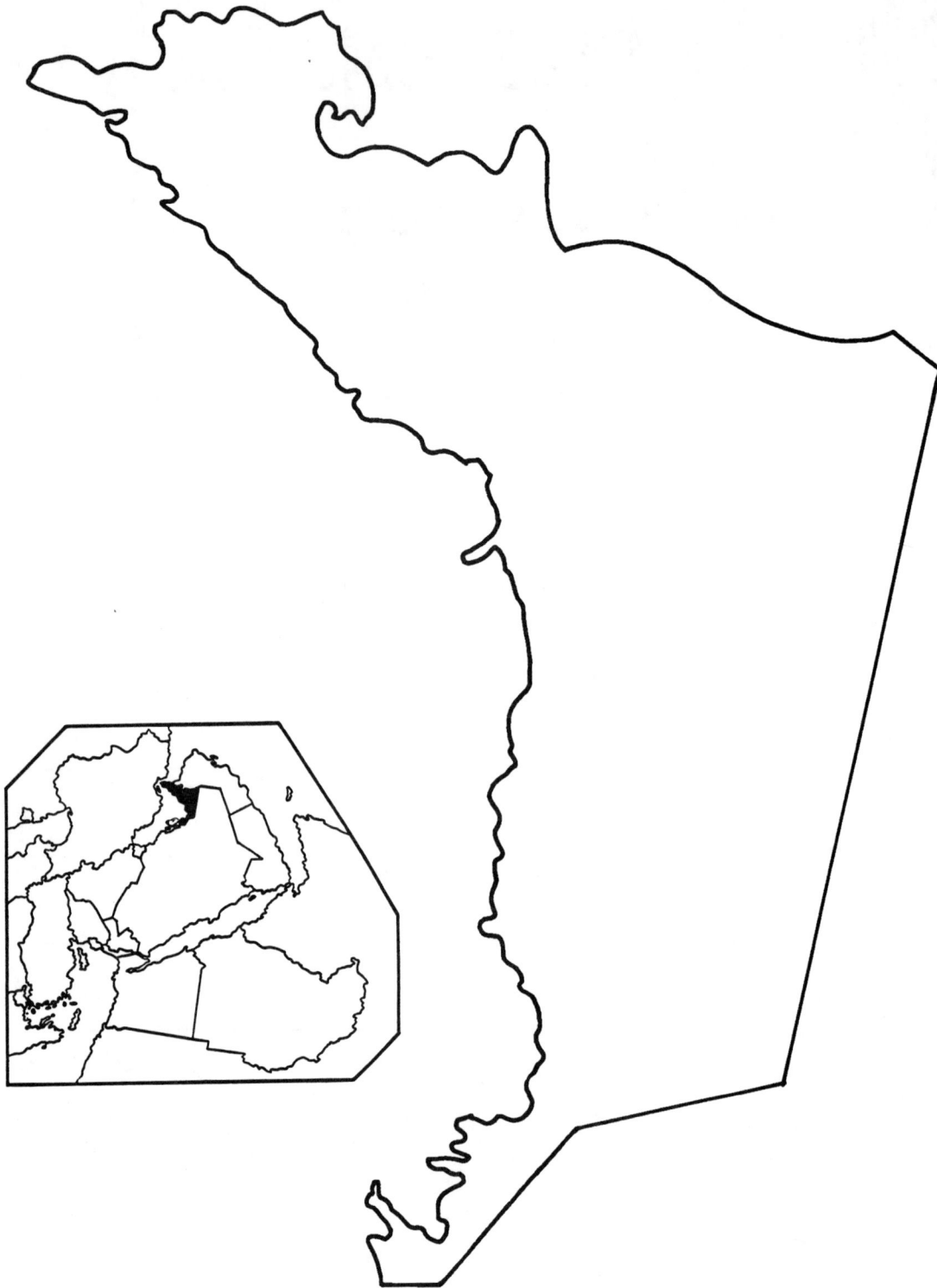

UNITED ARAB EMIRATES

UNITED ARAB EMIRATES

(YOO nih tid AHR ub EM ur uhts)

Name _____

Date _____

DATE of INDEPENDENCE: 1971.

NATION'S CAPITAL CITY: Abu Dhabi.

OFFICIAL LANGUAGE: Arabic.

FORM of GOVERNMENT: Republic.

AREA: 32,000 square miles (82,880 square kilometers).

POPULATION (est. 1989): 2,250,000 people.   _Density_: 70 people per square mile.
27 people per square kilometer.
77% urban (city) living and 23% rural (country) living.

LARGEST CITY: Abu Dhabi - 537,000 people.

ELEVATION: _Highest_: Jabal Yibir - 5,010 feet (1,527 m) above sea level.
Lowest: Salamiyah - slightly below below sea level.

ADDITIONAL INFORMATION: Before the mid-1900's and the discovery of oil, the region of the United Arab Emirates was one of the most underdeveloped in the world. • A ruler called an _emir_ governs each of the seven states, called _emirates_. • Many people living outside of the cities live in small **thatched** huts just as their ancestors did hundreds of years ago. • Desert **nomads** tend herds of camels, goats and sheep.

United Arab Emirates' Flag

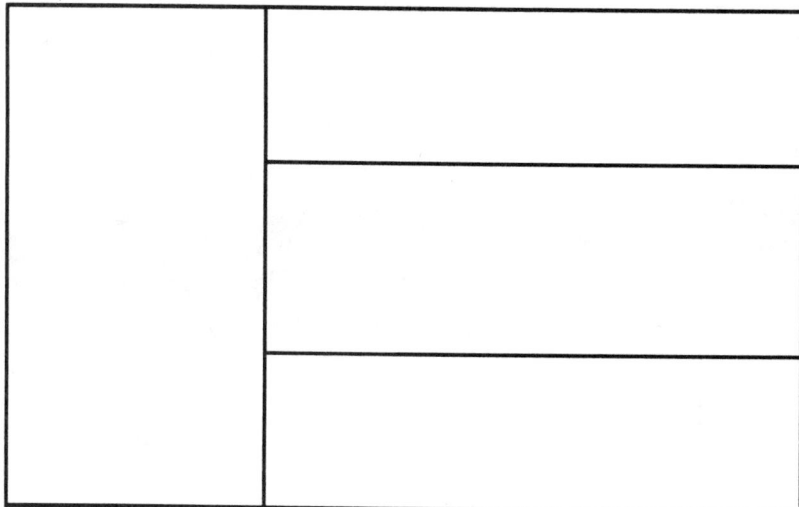

Flag Description

1. The top stripe is green; the bottom stripe is black; the center is white. (Several other Arab nations use the same colors for the stripes on their flags.)

2. The verticle stripe on the left is red.

3. The flag's four colors represent four periods in Arab history.

4. Color the flag the correct colors.

UNITED ARAB EMIRATES

Name _____

Date _____

EARLY HISTORY in BRIEF

The United Arab Emirates (UAE) is a federation of seven independent Arab states in the southwestern region of Asia. The seven states lie along the eastern coast of the Arabian Peninsula — along the Persian Gulf. The names of the seven states are 1.) Abu Dhabi, 2.) Al Fujayrah, 3.) Ash Shariqah, 4.) Dubayy, 5.) Ras al Khaymah, 6.) Ujman, and 7.) Umm al Qaywayn.

People have lived in the region that is now known as the United Arab Emirates for thousands of years. The chiefs of the Arab groups that first settled in the area gradually gained control of the region. During the A.D. 600's, is when most of the people living in the area converted to the Moslem religion.

These states are located along the major trade route between Europe and the nations of Eastern Asia. It was because of this **strategic** location that several European nations established trading posts in the area during the 1500's. The European nations **competed** with the Arabs, Persians and Turks for control of the gulf trade. Over a period of time, Great Britain became the most powerful European country in the gulf region.

British and local Arab ships often battled during the late 1700's and the early 1800's. Finally, in 1820, the Arab rulers of the Emirates and Britain signed a peace treaty that ended the fighting. The British and Arab leaders signed several other treaties over a period of years. Because they signed so many treaties, they came to be called the **Trucial States**. In time, Britain took control of the states' defenses and foreign affairs. However, the leaders of the Emirates continued to handle all of their **internal** affairs.

The Trucial States were underdeveloped until the mid-1900's, when foreign oil companies began to drill for oil in the region. However, they continued to rely on agriculture and fishing as important products in their economy.

It wasn't until 1971 that the Trucial States gained full independence from Great Britain. Even though the states had been long-time rivals, all of the states except Ras al Khaymah joined together and formed the United Arab Emirates. They formed the union on December 2, 1971. Ras al Khaymah finally joined in Emirates in February, 1972.

A gardener looks over his plants.

❑ ❑ ❑ ❑ ❑ ❑ ❑

UNITED ARAB EMIRATES

Name _____

Date _____

Circle each correct answer.

1. How many Arab states make up the United Arab Emirates?

    a. three   b. five   c. seven   d. nine

2. What year did the United Arab Emirates gain their independence?

    a. 1972   b. 1971   c. 1900   d. 1820

3. What year were all of the United Arab Emirates united?

    a. 1972   b. 1971   c. 1900   d. 1820

Fill in each blank with the correct answer.

4. The capital city of the United Arab Emirates is _____ .

5. _____ is the official language the United Arab Emirates.

6. _____ is the largest city in the United Arab Emirates.

7. From what country did the United Arab Emirates gain their independence?

_____

8. Explain why several European countries established trading posts in the region.

_____

_____

_____

_____

9. Explain why the United Arab Emirates came to be called the *Trucial States.*

_____

_____

Bonus ☆ ☆ ☆

Use another resource book and write a report on the Persian Gulf, the Moslem religion, the
British Empire, OPEC, or petroleum and/or the products made from petroleum.
Look in the newspaper and see if you can find current news about the UAE.
Include pictures and maps in your report if they are applicable.

Yemen

Map • Facts • History & Review Questions

New Words to Learn:

Find the words in a dictionary and write the meanings on the lines.

1. **chieftain** - _____

2. **imam** - _____.

3. **mass** - _____.

4. **overthrow** - _____.

5. **prosperity** - _____

6. **tattoo** - _____.

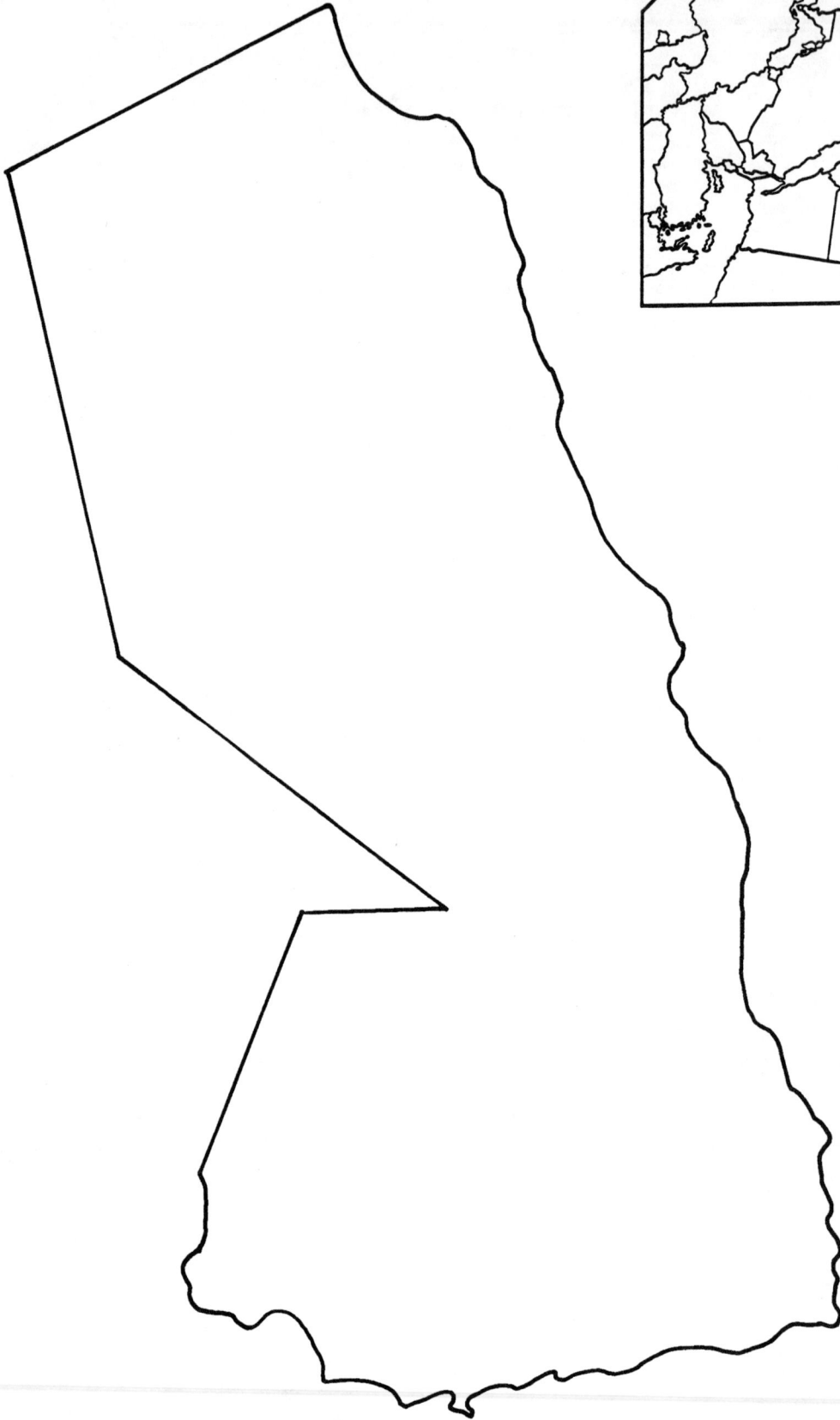

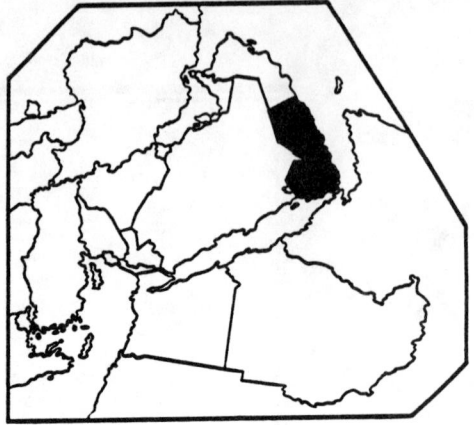

YEMEN

YEMEN
(YAY mihn)

DATE of INDEPENDENCE: 1967 (Aden); 1962 (Sana's republic established).

NATION'S CAPITAL CITY: Sana.

OFFICIAL LANGUAGE: Arabic.

FORM of GOVERNMENT: Republic.

AREA: 207,000 square miles (536,128 square kilometers).

POPULATION (est. 1989): 11,000,000 people.   _Density_: 53 people per square mile.
21 people per square kilometer.
37% urban (city) living and 63% rural (country) living.

LARGEST CITY: Sana - 427,000 people.

ELEVATION: _Highest_: Mt. Hadur Shuayb - 12,336 feet (3,760 m) above sea level.
Lowest: Sea level along the coast.

ADDITIONAL INFORMATION: On May 22, 1990, Yemen (Aden) and Yemen (Sana) united into one country. • The climate ranges from about 60° F. to 130° F. (15° to 54° C) • Oil is the most important industry in the southeastern part of the country (formerly Aden), while farming is the main source of income for the northern part of the country (formerly Sana). • Many of the women are **tattooed** on their faces and arms with tribal marks. • Only about 10% of the people can read and write.

Yemen's Flag

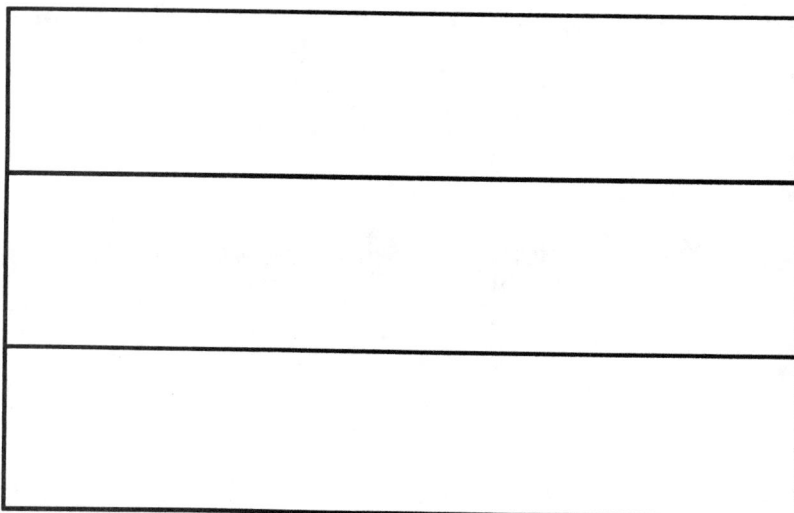

Flag Description

1. The top stripe is red; the bottom stripe is black; the center is white. (Several other Arab nations use the same colors for the stripes on their flags.)

2. Color the flag the correct colors.

YEMEN

Name _____

Date _____

EARLY HISTORY in BRIEF

Until May 22, 1990, Yemen was two separate countries. One was named *Yemen (Aden)* and the other was *Yemen (Sana)*.

According to Arab tradition, Semitic people invaded the region of today's Yemen about 2000 B.C. It is said that these Semitic people taught farming and building skills to the herdsmen living in Yemen.

In ancient times, southern Arabia grew very wealthy because it was along the most important trade routes between Europe, Asia, and Africa. About 1400 B.C., an important trade route began. Caravans carrying pearls and spices passed through Yemen. During this period, cities and castles were built. Dams for irrigation and other water usage were also built.

The famous Queen of Sheba ruled the Yemeni during the 900's B.C. She visited King Solomon of the Hebrew nation about 950 B.C. It wasn't until the A.D. 600's., Mohammed's son-in-law, Ali, introduced the Islamic religion to the people in the area of Yemen.

Yemen's **prosperity** ended after the time of Christ. The local **chieftains** fought among themselves and Ethiopian forces invaded Yemen. For over a century, fighting took place between Yemeni tribes and religious groups. They were also invaded several times by Egyptians and Turks. All of this conflict brought **mass** destruction to the region.

The Ottoman Empire controlled Yemen off and on from 1517 to 1918. The country, Yemen (Aden) became independent in 1918. However, Great Britain took control of the city of Aden in 1839. Aden (the city) became an important British refueling stop for ships going to India by way of the Suez Canal and the Red Sea. Aden was a part of the British Empire until 1937.

In 1962, a group of military officers who were supported by Egypt **overthrew** the **imam** and set up a republic in Yemen (Sana). The imam's forces — called *Royalists* — fought from the mountains to try and regain control of the country. Saudi Arabia supported the imam. However, the *Republicans*, who were supported by Egypt, controlled most of Yemen. The fighting between the republicans and the royalists ended in 1970.

Yemen (Sana) opposed Communism, while Yemen (Aden) favored Communism. The two countries fought several times over the border between them in the 1970's. An agreement uniting the two countries was signed on March 29, 1979. However, they remained separated until their formal unification on May 22, 1990.

❑ ❑ ❑ ❑ ❑ ❑ ❑ ❑ ❑ ❑ ❑

MIDDLE EAST: **Section 17** – 100

© GOLDEN EDUCATIONAL CENTER

YEMEN

REVIEW QUESTIONS   Date _____

Circle each correct answer.

1. What year did Yemen (Aden) and Yemen (Sana) unite?

    a. 1979   b. 1990   c. 1962   d. 1970

2. What year did Yemen (Aden) and Yemen (Sana) formally unite?

    a. 1979   b. 1990   c. 1962   d. 1970

Fill in each blank with the correct answer.

3. The capital city of Yemen is _____ .

4. _____ is the official language of Yemen.

5. Explain why southern Arabia came to be very wealthy in the 1400's.

    _____

    _____

    _____

    _____

    _____

6. Explain several of the ways that petroleum and petroleum products have changed our lives for the better and the worse. Be detailed. Use more paper if necessary.

    _____

    _____

    _____

    _____

    _____

    _____

    _____

    _____

Bonus ☆ ☆ ☆

Use another resource book and write a report on the Red Sea, OPEC, or Suez Canal.
Look in the newspaper and see if you can find current news about Yemen.
Include pictures and maps in your report if they are applicable.

MIDDLE EAST
Answer Keys

Section 1 - Bahrain (page 5)
1. a. 1971
2. c. Portugal
3. b. Persia
4. Great Britain
5. Manama
6. Portugal
7. direct say
8. Al Khalifeh Arabs
9. social welfare programs
10. protectorate
11. *Teacher Check*

Section 3 - Egypt (page 18)
1. birthplace of civilization
2. upper; lower
3. Cairo
4. pyramids; desert; tombs; pharaohs
5. 1922
6. armies; powerful; world
7. commercial cotton growing; British; dam; Cairo; irrigation canals; Delta
8. *Teacher Check*
9. *Teacher Check*

Section 2 - Cyprus (page 11)
1. a. Greek
2. c. Native
3. d. 1960
4. Greek; 1200 B.C.
5. Mediterranean Sea
6. political unrest
7. Republic
8. Nicosia
9. conquered; 1191; sold; French
10. Christianity
11. constitution; Greece; Turkey; Great Britain
12. *Teacher Check*

Section 4 - Iran (page 24)
1. d. Islam
2. d. Farsi
3. c. Islamic Republic
4. Teheran; population; largest
5. empire; 200; deliver; coins; money; irrigation
6. nomads
7. Persia; Greek; Persis
8. Always independent
9. *Teacher Check*

MIDDLE EAST

REVIEW ANSWERS

Section 5 - Iraq (page 29)
1. d. Great Britain
2. a. Arabic
3. d. Persian Gulf
4. 1932
5. Romans of Asia
6. Tigris; Euphrates; Mesopotamia
7. Noah
8. Assyria; Iraq
9. *Teacher Check*

Section 6 - Israel (page 35)
1. Romans; Palestine
2. May 22, 1948
3. persecuted (or slaughtered); Nazi Germany; migrated; Palestine; World War II
4. Hebrew; Arab; centuries
5. Palestine; independent
6. Jerusalem
7. Jerusalem
8. Mediterranean Sea
9. Jesus Christ; Bethlehem; Roman
10. *Teacher Check*

Section 7 - Jordan (page 41)
1. settlements; world; Jericho
2. Moslem Arabs;
3. Assyrians; Chaldeans; Egyptians; Persians
4. 1946
5. Great Britain
6. Transjordan
7. *Teacher Check*
8. *Teacher Check*

Section 8 - Kuwait (page 47)
1. *Teacher Check*

Section 9 - Lebanon (page 52)
1. a. France
2. a. 1948
3. a. Phoenicians
4. Istanbul
5. Mediterranean Sea
6. Mountains
7. Coastal
8. sailors; traders; explorer
9. *Teacher Check*

Section 10 - Oman (page 59)
1. b. 1500's
2. c. Arabian Peninsula
3. d. mid 1600's
4. Republic
5. Arabic
6. western; officially
7. Muscat
8. hottest; temperatures; high (or hot); six inches; year
9. Britain
10. *Teacher Check*

MIDDLE EAST

REVIEW ANSWERS

Section 11 - Qatar (page 66)
1. c. emir
2. a. 1971
3. a. Britain
4. Doha; population; largest
5. government; free; health care
6. Organization of Petroleum Exporting Countries
7. oil; main
8. *Teacher Check*
9. *Teacher Check*

Section 13 - Sudan (page 52)
1. a. by the Nile
2. b. Sennar
3. d. 1956
4. Khartoum
5. Arabic
6. Military
7. Great Britain
8. *Teacher Check*

Section 15 - Turkey (page 66)
1. a. 1876
2. c. Turkish
3. d. Ottoman
4. Ankara; Istanbul
5. Constantinople; Istanbul
6. Thrace; Anatolia
7. Turks; Ottomans; empire; Anatolia; Greece; Thrace; Ottoman Empire
8. *Teacher Check*

Section 12 - Saudi Arabia (page 69)
1. b. Bedouins
2. b. 1932
3. b. Moslem
4. Riyadh; population; largest
5. producers; exports
6. Arabic
7. *Teacher Check*
8. *Teacher Check*

Section 14 - Syria (page 59)
1. d. 1946
2. a. Arabic
3. c. 1200's B.C.
4. alphabet
5. Damascus
6. Syria; Lebanon; Palestine; Transjordon
7. *Teacher Check*

Section 16 - United Arab Emirates (page 69)
1. c. seven
2. b. 1971
3. a. 1972
4. Abu Dhabi
5. Arabic
6. Abu Dhabi
7. Great Britain
8. *Teacher Check*
9. *Teacher Check*

Section 17 - Yemen (page 75)
1. a. 1979
2. b. 1990
3. Sana
4. Arabic
5. *Teacher Check*
6. *Teacher Check*

golden educational center

"LEADING THE WAY IN CREATIVE EDUCATIONAL MATERIALS"™

SOUTH AMERICA
Country Studies

Reproducible
Maps,
Facts,
Histories &
Questions

Grade Level Range
See Back Cover

¡Hola!

RANDY L. WOMACK M.Ed.

CHRISTINA LEW

golden educational center

Country Study Materials

These books have a section on each of the independent countries of North and South America. Each section has a large country map, a page of current facts and interesting information, a short one or two page history through independence and one page of questions that can be answered with the information we provide. There is also an answer key for each section.

GEC-1965   **NORTH AMERICA Country Studies** (96 pages)
GEC-1975   **SOUTH AMERICA Country Studies** (96 pages)

The layout and information of these books are similar to North and South America. Each country or province has its own respective section. **Your kids will love the easy-to-use format!**

GEC-1935   **FAR EAST Country Studies** (112 pages)
GEC-1936   **MIDDLE EAST Country Studies**
GEC-1985   **CANADA Province Studies** (96 pages)

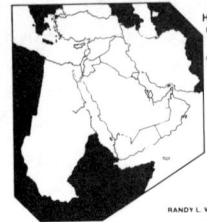

Middle East
Country Studies

Reproducible
Maps,
Facts,
Histories &
Questions

GRADE LEVEL RANGE
See Back Cover

RANDY L. WOMACK M.Ed.

CHRISTINA LEW

golden educational center

U.S. Outline Maps

Reproducible
Maps, Facts
& Questions

Grade Level Range
See Back Cover

golden educational center
LEADING THE WAY IN CREATIVE EDUCATIONAL MATERIALS

U.S. Outline Maps & State Studies

This 112 page book has an individual Fact Sheet and Outline Map for each of the 50 states, Washing-ton D.C., and the entire U.S. U.S. Waterway and State Bound-ary Maps are also included. The question and research activity pages can be used with each of the states.

GEC-1992

U.S. Geography

The sections of this 80 page book include a World Overview, Physical, Economical, and Political Features as well as Climate information. Maps, activities and questions are included in each section. There is even a review section for the entire book. **This book has a unique, easy-to-use (and read) format that you and your students will enjoy!**

GEC-1993

U.S. Geography

Grade Level Range
See Back Cover

RANDY L. WOMACK M.Ed.
Author

CHRISTINA LEW
Artist

golden educational center

Continent Maps & Studies

Reproducible
Continent Maps
Facts & Questions

Grade Level Range
See Back Cover

golden educational center

Continent Maps & Studies

This book contains an Outline, Waterway, and Political Boundary Map and Individual Fact Sheet for all of the continents. There are questions, research activities and a glossary that can be used with each of continent section. World Maps and answer Keys are also included.

GEC-1905

Learning the Continents

Africa, Asia, Europe, North America and South America each have a 16 page section of maps & activities. Students use maps to identify, memorize and locate the countries, waterways, and points of interest on each continent. A word search is also included.

GEC-1906

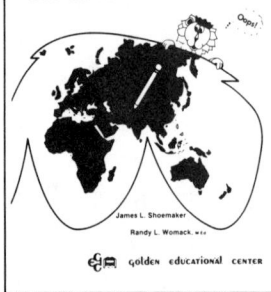

Learning the Continents

Reproducible
Maps, Lessons
& Questions

Grade Level Range
See Back Cover

Oops!

James L. Shoemaker
Randy L. Womack M.Ed.

golden educational center

"JUMBO" REPRODUCIBLE MAPS

These 11x17" maps are printed on card stock.
Continent Maps
GEC-1998 - **1 each of 8 Outline Maps**

GEC-1999 - **1 each of 8 Political Boundary Maps**
U.S. • N. America • Europe • Africa • S. America • Asia • Australia • World.
$10.00 per package

GEC-1996 - **North America Political Boundaries Pack**
N. America • Canada • United States • Mexico - Central America

GEC-1997 - **Eastern Continents Political Boundaries Pack**
World (Pacific View) • Asia • Far East • Middle East
$5.95 per package

U.S. Word Search and State Studies

This 112 page book has a large word search map for each state. Each state also has an interesting fact and short history sheet that can be used to facilitate more research about the respective state.

GEC-1915

U.S. WORD SEARCH & STATE STUDIES

Reproducible
Activity
Sheets

RANDY L. WOMACK M.Ed.
JAMES L. SHOEMAKER
SHARON JACKSON

golden educational